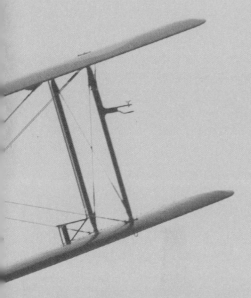

LEGENDS OF WARFARE

AVIATION

Spad Fighters

The Spad A.2 to XVI in World War I

MARK C. WILKINS

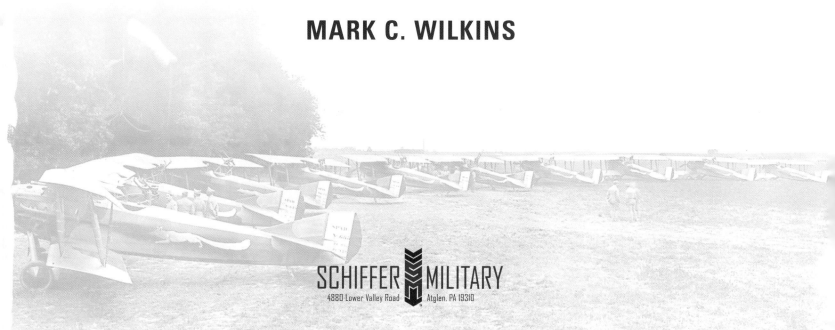

SCHIFFER MILITARY

4880 Lower Valley Road   Atglen, PA 19310

Type set in Impact/Minion Pro/Univers LT Std
Front and rear cover images courtesy of David Trost

ISBN: 978-0-7643-5665-0
Printed in China

Published by Schiffer Publishing, Ltd.
4880 Lower Valley Road
Atglen, PA 19310
Phone: (610) 593-1777; Fax: (610) 593-2002
E-mail: Info@schifferbooks.com
www.schifferbooks.com

For our complete selection of fine books on this and related subjects, please visit our website at www.schifferbooks.com. You may also write for a free catalog.

Schiffer Publishing's titles are available at special discounts for bulk purchases for sales promotions or premiums. Special editions, including personalized covers, corporate imprints, and excerpts, can be created in large quantities for special needs. For more information, contact the publisher.

We are always looking for people to write books on new and related subjects. If you have an idea for a book, please contact us at proposals@schifferbooks.com.

Acknowledgments

I would like to thank the following individuals for their invaluable help with this book: Michael O'Neal, president of the League of World War I Aviation Historians; the staff of the Golden Age Air Museum; Andy Parks, president of the Vintage Aero Museum; Clay Hammond, vice president and chief pilot for the Old Rhinebeck Aerodrome; Sarah E. Dunne, archivist and librarian for the Owls Head Transportation Museum; and Ted Huetter, senior manager, Public Relations and Promotions, for the Museum of Flight. Many thanks too to the staff at the National Archives and Record Administration.

"Our machines, groomed for flight, stood in front of the hangars, the motors purring softly, propellers 'idling over' at 350 revolutions. Machines, motors—one uses the words reluctantly. Machines they never were, those little Spads. Call them zincs or coucous, the French pilot's terms of endearment."

—James Norman Hall, *My Island Home*, p. 196.

Contents

The Société pour l'Aviation et ses Dérivés (SPAD)

Louis Béchereau, who would eventually design the Spad aircraft, was a gifted designer who showed a facility for mechanisms and structures at an early age. He attended the École Nationale Professionelle located in Vierzon. Next he studied at the Arts et Métiers in Angers in 1896—completing his studies in 1901. Interestingly, he won first prize in a model competition organized by L'Auto. This model was then produced for Parisian department stores. Béchereau then enlisted in the army and was discharged in 1902.

Béchereau then worked on the development of a prototype car of Clement Ader's design in a factory in Bezons. He took a number of trial flights with the Ader Éole or Avion. In 1902, Ader's nephew created the Société de Construction d'Appareils Aeriens, and in 1909, Armand Deperdussin placed an order for an airplane that was exhibited in Paris (Bon Marche). The following year Deperdussin founded the Société de Production des Aéroplanes Deperdussin (SPAD). In 1911, Béchereau approached Deperdussin with a revolutionary new design for a racer—shortly thereafter, he secured Béchereau as his chief designer (Hare 1937, 1).

It could be said that Béchereau had a fascination both with speed and ruggedness from the outset. It was Béchereau who conceived and developed the idea for a monocoque fuselage—which was more akin to boatbuilding than airplane construction. This would serve two functions: it would allow a streamlined fuselage with very little internal bracing—the load being carried by the skin of the form ("stressed skin"). It was both lightweight and strong. The Deperdussin Racer of 1912, piloted by Jules Vedrines, won the Gordon Bennett trophy for speed—the sleek little racer attaining 107.4 mph—unheard of for the time (Hare 1937, 1).

Deperdussin fell into bankruptcy in 1913 due to malfeasance; the company went into administration and the name was changed to Société Provisoire des Aéroplanes Deperdussin—the SPAD acronym was born. Income ceased after Deperdussin's disgrace, resulting in uncertainty for SPAD. Louis Blériot spearheaded a consortium that bought up the company's assets in 1913. The new company was renamed the Société pour l'Aviation et Ses Dérivés, which allowed the retention of the SPAD acronym. More important was the retention of the company's chief asset: Louis Béchereau, who would go on to design the famous Spad VII and XIII.

It is also important to understand the context in which the Spads were developed—and this was largely a combination of competing with German aircraft and pilot reports of what worked and what didn't during aerial combat. With the advent of the Albatros series of aircraft, the Allies were left somewhat disadvantaged—the Nieuports were still more maneuverable, but the Albatroses had a tougher fuselage owing to its semimonocoque construction, a Mercedes 160 hp in-line liquid-cooled engine (straight 6), and dual machine guns. The Pfalz fighters were similar to the Albatros fighters except they had a slightly better rate of climb and were structurally a little tougher. The Spad fighter was an effort to increase ruggedness and speed of the French pursuit planes and eventually more firepower—it also mirrored the German trend toward in-line engines, making a break with the rotaries that had characterized the Nieuports and early Fokker and Pfalz aircraft.

A Spad that survived the Great War— 93rd Aero Squadron Spad XIII is pictured at Foucaucourt Airdrome, France, in November 1918. The stripes on upper left wing would have been common to all Spads of this period and would have been alternately red, green, red, green, red. Also visible is a bomb rack just between the gear legs, which was indicative of late-war ground support missions. This may be S.7799, piloted by Capt. Robert Rockwell. The blue cowling with the white edging indicates that this aircraft was from C flight. *NARA*

185th Aero Spad XIII, assigned to Lt. Arthur Truscott from New Jersey, coded "2" and thought to be serial number S.18805. Seen in the cockpit is squadron CO Jerry Vasconcells, who was credited with six victories. The Unit was a night-fighter unit—hence the "bat and moon" insignia. The unit originally flew Sopwith Camels, but was then reequipped with Spads during the postwar period. This aircraft was later destroyed when a D.H. 4 careened into a line of 185th Spads during landing at the 185th field at Grand Vosges on March 29, 1919. *NARA*

CHAPTER 1

Nieuports and the Need for a New Fighter

The Nieuport line of fighters began with the Nieuport 10 and then continued with the Nieuport 11, which was originally designed by Gustave Delage as a racing plane for the Gordon Bennett Trophy race of 1913. After the outbreak of war during the summer of 1914, all peacetime plans for aircraft ceased as designers and military officials focused on how best to fit these new machines for war. Initial aerial efforts were skewed toward reconnaissance and observation for artillery—but pilots in opposing aircraft quickly progressed toward combat. Pilots in passing aircraft initially waved, nasty gestures were next, and this was followed by shoes being thrown—then pistol shots, culminating with the fitting of machine guns to airframes of both sides.

With the advent of Anthony Fokker's E series of monoplanes, or *Eindeckers*, the Allies were caught off guard—the French and British had nothing like this at this time, and the *Eindeckers* with synchronized machine guns wreaked havoc on Allied aircraft. The *Eindecker* still had wing warping—a throwback to the Wright Brothers—but it had a machine gun synchronized to fire through the propeller—the entire aircraft became a "point and shoot" weapon. The magazine for these guns held 250 rounds, as compared to the Lewis guns fitted on Allied planes, which held only forty-six rounds. The Allies scrambled to come up with a fighter that could best the *Eindecker* in this regard, and the answer was the Nieuport 11. The nimble and lightly built Nieuport 11 was superior to the *Eindecker* in every way except for armament—the Allies still hadn't worked out the synchronizing gear. Their solution was to mount a Lewis gun atop the upper plane that simply fired over the prop. The Nieuport 11 quickly turned the tide in favor of the Allies, and these planes were rushed into production and delivered to frontline service quickly. The Nieuport 17 followed during March 1916—it had a 110 hp Le Rhône engine, a slightly larger wingspan and fuselage, and, most importantly—a synchronized Vickers machine gun that fired through the prop. By November 1916, the Germans had introduced the Albatros line of fighters—these had two synchronized machine gun that fired through the prop using the Alkan-Hamy synchronizing gear. The Allies needed something that could best the Albatros.

The Nieuport 11 was the first real fighter aircraft that the Allies possessed—it was the F-16 of the day. The Allies had not solved the interrupter gear problem yet, so a .303 Lewis gun was mounted on top of the upper plane—it simply fired over the arc of the propeller. The Lewis gun had a forty-seven-round magazine that the pilot had to change while still flying the plane—which was not easy! *Author*

The Fokker *Eindecker* E.III was an interesting aircraft in that it possessed some very old elements such as wing warping, patented by the Wright brothers, and some very innovative elements such as the synchronized machine gun, which allowed it to fire through the propeller without hitting it. It was popularized both by Max Immelmann and Oswald Boelcke—two early German aces. Immelmann developed his famous turn—a steep climbing turn followed by a hard right or left rudder (what is today known as a stall turn)—in an *Eindecker*, which, given their sensitivity on the elevator and rudder, was no small feat. Add to this the sluggishness of wing warping, the gyroscopic effect imparted by the rotary engine, and the context of early dogfighting. *Public domain*

Dutchman Anthony Fokker—who originally offered his services to the Allies—became one of the driving forces behind aircraft design and production in Germany. During the early war, the debate raged between the monoplane and biplane for the preeminent type for fighter or chase or pursuit aircraft. The Morane Saulnier Type H was one of the best French fighters, and it was from a captured one that Fokker derived the idea for the Fokker *Eindecker*. This plane was a quantum leap forward in that it had a synchronized Spandau machine gun that could fire through the propeller—without hitting it! *Public domain*

A Le Rhône 9J rotary 110 hp engine. Note how the intake manifolds are mounted behind the crankcase on the 110 and in front on the 80 hp. The 110 was more powerful but not as trouble free as the 80 hp version. Le Rhône 9J engines were produced under license in Great Britain by W. H. Allen Son & Company of Bedford, and in Germany by Motorenfabrik Oberursel. The German version was termed the Oberursel UR.II. The 110 powered not only the Nieuport 17, but also the Avro 504, Fokker Dr. 1, the Sopwith Pup, and many others. *Public domain*

With the advent of the Nieuport 17, the Alkan-Hamy interrupter gear had been invented, which allowed a Vickers .303 machine gun to be mounted atop the cowling in front of the pilot. This interrupter gear was developed by *Sergeant-Mecanicien* Robert Alkan and *l'Ingenieur du Maritime* Hamy. It was derived from the Fokker Stangensteuerung gear; however, it was different in that the pushrod was installed within the Vickers gun. This mitigated a major drawback of other pushrod gears in that the rod, being supported for its whole length, was much less prone to distortion or breakage. Some units kept the Lewis gun on the top wing (British Nieuports retained this gun uniformly). The N-17 was a bit bigger with a 110 Le Rhône rotary, a slightly larger wingspan to make it easier for new pilots to fly. *Public domain*

A Nieuport 17 C.1 at Langley Field, Virginia, being inspected by Lt. E. LeMaitre and Capt. J. C. Bartolf. Note the two holes in the bottom of the cowling—the holes allowed the cylinders to be primed in order to start the engine. The large V strut of the Nieuport supported the two wing spars in the upper wing, and the single spar in the lower wing. *Library of Congress 09329*

LeMaitre and Bartolf appear to be examining how the interrupter gear functions; one of them is turning the prop and the other appears to be examining the Vickers gun. Note how minimal the rigging is relative to the Spad. This is one reason why Nieuports could lose their wings in a dive. Also note the bungee cords, which serve as shock absorbers for the landing gear. *Library of Congress 09343*

The Nieuport 11, 16, and 17 all shared one common flaw: the lower wing had only one spar, which meant that it was vulnerable to attack (one well-placed burst of an enemy machine gun) and to failing during a high-speed dive. Because the Nieuports were lightly built, they were extremely maneuverable. The lower wing spar is faintly visible in this photograph, about one-third of the distance back from the leading edge of the lower wing. *Library of Congress 09334*

Nieuport 17s lined up on the flight line at Issoudun. Note that the Vickers machine guns have been removed, and, interestingly, these aircraft have mudguards on the landing gear to prevent mud from splashing up onto the upper wings and fuselage. These aircraft were used for training hence the large black numbers painted on the fuselage. *NARA 530721*

A replica Nieuport 17 C.1 built by Robert Gould-Gallier in *Lafayette Escadrille* colors. This aircraft was used in the filming of the movie *Flyboys. Public domain*

A captured Albatros DV. The Germans had developed the Albatros line of fighters, which featured a rugged semimonocoque fuselage (internal formers sheathed by panels made of compound-curved plywood), two synchronized machine guns, and a 160 hp in-line Mercedes engine—this was important, since the in-line liquid-cooled Mercedes did not have the gyroscopic effect found in every aircraft with a rotary engine. These important attributes were not lost on the Allies and resulted in a critical eye being cast toward the much-beloved but fragile Nieuport and Sopwith and Pup fighters. *Library of Congress 4639-6*

A model of an Albatros D. III flying. The D. III incorporated design traits of the very successful Nieuports—like the sesquiplane wing arrangement. In doing this, the Germans transferred the Nieuport's fatal flaw—the single spar in the lower wing—to their aircraft. That being said, the D. III was an excellent all-around fighter. *Model and photo by author*

CHAPTER 2
Early Spads

The S.A.1 and S.A.2 were largely a desire to work around the lack of an interrupter gear that allowed the machine gun to fire through the propeller. It was a tractor that combined the forward-firing ability of the DH 2 with a tractor 80 hp Le Rhône 9C rotary engine arrangement. It featured box girder construction with a rounded aft turtle deck and aluminum and plywood panels around the cockpit and engine. It was awkward and extremely dangerous, to say the least, since the gunner's head was a few inches from the spinning prop! The A.1 was flown for the first time on May 21, 1915 (Kowalski 2007, 9). Its performance was noted as being better than contemporaneous pusher designs, so an order was placed for eleven S.A.1s by the French air force (Kowalski 2007, 9). The SA.2 had a shorter wingspan, and a redesigned pair of air scoops flanking the engine—since the nacelle blocked the cooling air that usually was allowed to flow over the whirling rotary. Forty-two S.A.2s were delivered to the Aviation Militaire, and fifty-seven were built for Russia (Kowalski 2007, 9). S.A.3, S.A.4, and S.A.5 variants were built, each having marginal improvements; these aircraft were not very popular, and the following report by England in 1916 summarized the problems: "In this machine the passenger is slung in a small fuselage in front of a tractor propeller. This arrangement is considered to be unnecessarily dangerous and the objects attained as regards arc of fire do not justify it. All the Spad machines are of similar type and are considered to be of no interest in their present form." (Kowalski 2007, 10). Russian pilots liked them well enough to continue using the A.2s and A.4s until 1921.

Specifications for the S.A. 1 and S.A. 2		
	S.A. 1	**S.A. 2**
Span:	31 ft. 4 in. (9.55 m)	31 ft. 4 in. (9.55 m)
Length:	23 ft. 11 in. (7.29 m)	25 ft. 9 in. (7.85 m)
Height:	8 ft. 6.5 in. (2.60 m)	8 ft. 6.5 in. (2.60 m)
Wing area:	273 ft.^{2} (25.36 m^2)	273 ft.^{2} (25.36 m^2)
Weight empty:	928 lbs. (421 kg)	913 lbs. (414 kg)
Weight loaded:	1,562 lbs. (708 kg)	1,485 lbs. (674 kg)
Maximum speed:	84 mph (135 km/h) at sea level	87 mph (140 km/h) at sea level
Climb:	to 3,282 ft. (1,000 m) in 6 min. 30 sec.	
Endurance:	2 hr. 45 min.	3 hr.
Max Range (mi)	740	1,800
Ceiling (ft)	30,000	32,600
Total production	1	285

Evident in this design are some Spad features that would carry through to the XIII; for example, the wings look similar to the later Spad VII and include the unique Spad system of bracing—two interplane struts outboard with antivibration struts (not true interplane struts) inboard. This was the direct result of complaints from Nieuport pilots regarding the weakness of Nieuport cellule structure in a dive. Also included in the A.2 wings was the system of actuating the ailerons by means of bell cranks and pushrods, which would carry through to the Spad XIII. The rudder and vertical fin on the A2 bear a resemblance to the later Spad fins, as does the robust landing gear. *"Rapaceone" Creative Commons Attribution— Share Alike 3.0 Unported license*

Pictured is Spad S.A. 1, serial number 1, photographed at Chalons, France, in 1915. This was the first production model of this type. It differs from the final production version of the S.A. 1 in that the engine cowling resembles that of the prototype. Also, the fitting at the top of the gun track is different from the final configuration seen in the production S.A. 1. This aircraft was sent to *Escadrille MS 23* during the summer of 1915. *Capitaine* Maurice Schlumberger was the pilot, and *Capitaine* Max Boucher was the gunner/observer who occupied the front cockpit. Schlumberger was killed in action on November 15, 1915, in Spad S.A. 1 serial S. 10. *Greg Van Wyngarden*

"Ma Jeanne" was an A.2 of the French air force. Clearly visible in this image is the propeller and engine behind the gunner in the forward nacelle. This nacelle pivoted near the landing-gear spreader bar to allow it to drop down to service the 80 hp Le Rhône rotary engine. This configuration was a compromise solution to the lack of an effective interrupter gear and the desire for a tractor biplane. Perhaps the best part of this fighter was that it allowed Béchereau to realize what didn't work (the forward gunner position in front of the prop) and take the best features of this plane to produce the Spad VII. *Greg VanWyngarden*

This image depicts Spad S.A. 1, serial number 17 (painted on rudder), that displays the French tricolor bars on the fuselage instead of the more typical French cockades. This particular aircraft features a hooked horn-like stanchion for the gun mount immediately behind the front gunner's cockpit and head, which may have afforded more protection (or perceived protection) for the gunner/observer, or provided more stability for the gun mount. *Greg Van Wyngarden*

An image of an 80 hp Le Rhône engine with crankcase face plate removed, of the type used in Nieuport 11s, Avro 504s, Sopwith Pups, and Spad A.2s. It was a 667-cubic-inch, nine-cylinder rotary engine that produced 1,200 rpm. It weighed approximately 268 lbs. and was produced in large quantities in France and Sweden. The lightweight 80 hp Le Rhône used less castor oil and gas than the Gnome rotaries, idled smoothly at low rpm, and was less expensive to produce. *Author*

An image of a Spad A.2 with the nose cupola rotated down, revealing the Le Rhône 80 hp engine. The cupola was fitted with an interesting gun armature for the Lewis gun, enabling the gun to be both swiveled and elevated upward of 90 degrees. Note the cage and headrest, which was all that stood between the gunner's head and the propeller blade! *Greg VanWyngarden*

A Spad A.3 in a hangar. Note that the pilot and gunner sit in their respective cockpits, and the gunner is wearing a padded training helmet—an extra bit of protection from that spinning prop just a few inches from his head. The pilot also has a gun fitted to an armature facing aft; presumably he could defend himself this way from a rear attack, although he'd have to shoot and fly the plane simultaneously which was no small feat as the Le Rhône had no throttle in the modern sense, but a mixture control for gas and air which required constant attention. It appears as though both guns in this image may be dummies—perhaps designers and mechanics were working out final armament placement for the A.2. The rear-facing gun does not appear on other images of the A.2 or subsequent models. *Greg VanWyngarden*

The Spad VII reproduction of the Old Rhinebeck Aerodrome seen doing a close pass for the photographer. Note the huge difference between the look of this aircraft versus the A series; much of the wing, fuselage, and tail structure have been refined, but this aircraft owes its lineage to the clumsy origins of the As. *David Trost, Old Rhinebeck Aerodrome volunteer*

Realizing that the A.2 through A.5 would never be a very successful fighter, Béchereau drastically modified his cumbersome and dysfunctional design, slashing away the worst aspects of the A series—primarily the nose. What he needed was a new type of engine, and Swiss engineer Marc Birkigt was the answer. Birkigt designed the first cast-aluminum engine block for the Hispano-Suiza automobile and engineering company in 1904 (steel cylinder sleeves were then fitted into the block), which yielded a light and powerful in-line engine, and it also allowed the genesis of the Spad VII. In 1914, Birkigt modified the engine for aviation use. The Spad VII was built around the Birkigt's V-8 engine. The fuselage was largely retained from aft of the cockpit to the empennage—which was refined and reconfigured, with the wings shortened, since now there was only one pilot, and the entire nose section was redesigned to house the 150 hp Hispano-Suiza 8Aa engine in a streamlined cowling. The undercarriage was simplified because now there was less weight to carry, and a single machine gun was placed just off-center to the right, allowing the pilot to sight down its length. Obviously, the invention of the Birkigt interrupter gear allowed this arrangement. The VII had a box girder fuselage with curved formers on the top and bottom, giving it a pleasing look. The sides also featured a slight curving, which was a nice break from the slab-sided Nieuports. The cowling panels were aluminum and featured many louvers, in an attempt to solve the finicky cooling problems of the Hissos. The wings were composed of thin airfoil ribs, with rounded lightening holes slid on to two main routed spars. The leading edge was sheathed with perforated plywood, and the trailing edge was wire—when the fabric was shrunk tight, it imparted the scalloped effect. Some Spads had linen or flax cord instead of wire on the trailing edge (Tallman 1973, 76). Instrumentation in the cockpit included a tachometer; airspeed, water temperature, and oil pressure gauges; and a compass. The fuel gauge was on the floor right over the belly tank, and the rest of the instruments were arranged like so many curios on a shelf-like apron that wrapped around the pilot. The Spads had straight sticks and featured a bell crank and pushrod aileron actuation system that was very effective; Frank Tallman noted that it imparted "a light feel and quick response" (Tallman, 1973, 76).

Specifications for the Spad VII 150 hp	
Span, upper plane	25 ft. 6 in.
Span, lower plane	25 ft. 6 in.
Chord, both planes	4 ft. 7 in.
Gap between planes	4 ft. 2 in.
Overall length	20 ft.
Total weight	1,525 lbs.
Useful load	470 lbs.
Climb in ten minutes	9,300 ft.
Speed at sea level	132 mph
Speed at 3,000 meters	126 mph
Engine	Hispano-Suiza "V" type, 150 hp

From "The Spad Scout,"
Flight, August 16, 1917

Pictured is the Hispano-Suiza automobile engine in a Grand Prix racer at Dieppe in 1912. Hispano-Suiza was founded in 1898 by Emilio de la Cuadra and Swiss engineer Marc Birkigt and was originally called La Cuadra. It produced autos and engines and changed hands and name between 1903 and 1904, finally settling on La Hispano-Suiza Fábrica de Automóviles—owned by José María Castro Fernández, with Birkigt as chief designer. The outbreak of the war and the rise of aviation compelled Birkigt to turn his attention to building high-performance yet lightweight aircraft engines. *Bibliothèque Nationale de France, public domain*

The Spad VII was deployed to frontline service in the fall of 1916. Aces such as George Guynemer were quick to realize the potential of this new machine. The Spad VII marked a shift not only in design, but in tactics. Prior to the Spad, the French air force and Royal Flying Corps (RFC) were using the nimble and lightly built Nieuport 17, which was an excellent turn fighter—meaning that they weren't fast but they could maneuver very effectively. In these early dogfights, maneuvering to a position on your opponent's tail was critical and became standard practice—so if you could turn in a tighter radius than your foe, you would have the upper hand. The Spad didn't turn as well as the Nieuport, but it was faster and more rugged. It could also stand up to dives at extreme speed, whereas if a Nieuport tried this, it would shed its lower wings (at the very least) due to their single-spar construction. Many a pilot's life was saved by simply diving his Spad away at high speed from an unfavorable engagement.

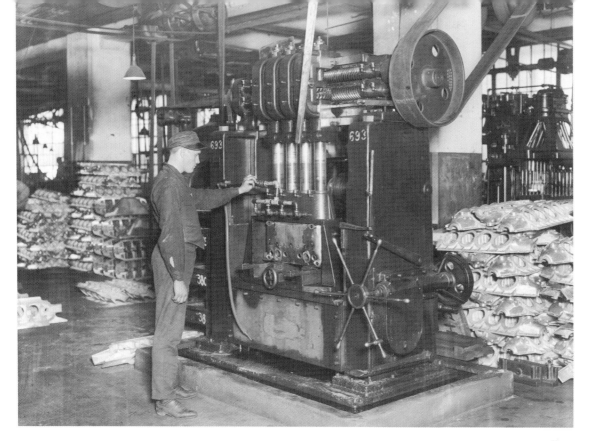

Hispano-Suiza apparently licensed Wright-Martin Aircraft Corporation to build their aircraft engines in the United States. Depicted in the image is a "Moline 4 spindle-boring machine" engaged in boring the four cylinders, and facing the bottoms of each, which will comprise half the cylinders in the Hispano-Suiza engine. *NARA 165-WW-4A-5*

Steel cylinder sleeves being machined. These fit inside the bored cast-aluminum blocks and provided the necessary strength where it was needed most, yet they kept the engine block light due to the aluminum casting. *NARA 165-WW-4A-09*

A "Fox multiple drilling machine," which simultaneously drills sixteen holes for the upper half of the crank case of the Hispano-Suiza V-8 engine. Note the drilling lubricant feed lines on each drill bit. *NARA 165 WW-4A-4*

The finished Hispano-Suiza engine, capable of between 150 hp and, in later models, 220 hp. The engine depicted in the image is a 180 hp—probably the best of the "Hisso" engines in terms of power-to-weight ratio and ease of maintenance. *USAF Museum, Wright Patterson, Ohio*

A cutaway of the Hispano-Suiza V-8 180 hp, showing the crankshaft, pistons, intake and exhaust manifolds, and valve gears. Also note the cams, which actuate the valve timing over the cylinders, which is in turn geared to the crankshaft—the engine thus worked reciprocally. *Brussels Museum*

Although this is a 200 hp Hispano-Suiza engine mounted on a Spad XIII airframe, it is clearly evident that the Spad fuselage was built around the engine, so carefully is it fitted with no room to spare. *NARA 165-WW-15D-18*

The finished Spad VII aircraft. Note the thin airfoils on the wings, the robust rigging, and unique exhaust stacks and cowling. This picture must have been taken in warmer weather, given the open side vents in the cowling. Keeping the "Hisso" engine at the proper temperature in various altitudes and weather conditions proved problematic. The Spad VII underwent four major cowling-facing versions: the first had a very small opening, allowing only a small amount of air to the radiator. The second version had nine holes pierced on the upper portion of the cowling face—from 9 o'clock to 3 o'clock, so to speak. The third version featured an enlarged cowling opening, and the late model featured the movable louvers that became standard on the Spad XIII. There were many other variations employed in the field in an effort to regulate the temperature of the engine. *NARA 18-WP-12918*

Gunsight →

*Instrument is available as a field mod

Aldis Sight*

Le-Chrétien Sight*

Clock

Altimeter

Fuel Tank Selector

Air Pump
Emergency Shutoff →

Oil
Pressure

Water
Temperature

Air Pump
Selector / Release

Magneto
Switches

Tachometer

Air Pressure
Regulator

Throttle

Anemometer*

Trigger

Mixture

Magneto
Starter

Cockpit Lamp*

Fuel Gauge

Compass

This is a graphic representation of the cockpit of an early Spad with the 150 hp Hispano-Suiza engine. It is fairly minimal, and of note is the spool directly in front of the pilot, under the "apron," upon which the ammunition for the Vickers gun was coiled. The empty belt traveled past the pilot's left arm on the apron and was coiled on a "take-up reel" aft and to the left of the pilot's seat. The forward windscreen had a hinged portion and latch that could be opened to clear jams in the breech of the Vickers gun.
Image courtesy Rise of Flight

FROM OTHER LANDS.
THE SPAD SCOUT.

IMPROVEMENT is so rapid and changes so frequent in the design of the Spads, developed by the Société Anonyme pour l'Aviation et ses Derivés, Paris, that the type used within the next few months may differ in several respects from that in use to-day. The accompanying drawing shows the outlines of the type " S. VII," which is said to be one of the most recent. Fighting craft of this type are piloted by members of the Lafayette Escadrille, and used with good effect equipped with one and sometimes two Lewis or Vickers machine-guns.

Approximate general dimensions of the " S. VII " are as follows :—

Span, upper plane	..	..	25 ft. 6 ins.
Span, lower plane	..	..	25 ft. 6 ins.
Chord, both planes	..	..	4 ft. 7 ins.
Gap between planes	..	..	4 ft. 2 ins.
Overall length	..	..	20 ft. 0 ins.
Total weight	..	..	1,525 lbs.
Useful load	..	..	470 lbs.
Climb in 10 minutes	..	..	9,300 ft.
Speed at sea level	..	..	132 m.p.h.
Speed at 3,000 metres	..	..	126 m.p.h.
Motor, Hispano-Suiza " V." type	..	160 h.p.

Both planes are nearly rectangular in plan, the ends being square and not raked, with corners slightly rounded off. The deep cut-out portion of the top plane, over the pilot's seat, as well as the close spacing of the interplane struts, shows a large area of plane surface aft of rear wing beams. As the *ailerons* are comparatively narrow, they must be carried on a subsidiary wing spar located about 9 ins. back of the main beam.

It will be noticed that the interplane bracing is unusual ; the wires from each side of the *fuselage* extend directly to the end struts, crossing at the intermediate struts. Where the wires cross there is a steel tube brace connecting the forward with rear intermediate wing struts.

The *fuselage* is exceptionally deep, and the bottom is curved below the lower *longerons* as well as the sides and top, giving a smooth stream-line effect. The fore end of the machine, which houses the motor, is covered with aluminium, with a circular radiator opening which resembles the cowling of a rotary motor. Protuberances on either side of the cowl show where the camshaft covers of the Hispano-Suiza motor project. Perforations are made in the cowling, about the motor projections, for the admission of air.

Wheels of the landing gear have a track of 5 ft. ; the axle runs in slots which guide it up and backward in line with the rear chassis struts. Shock absorption is with rubber cord.

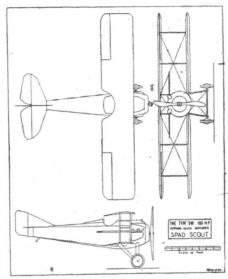

THE TYPE 30 160 H.P.
HISPANO-SUIZA MOTORED
SPAD SCOUT

The Hispano-Suiza motor develops 160 h.p. at about 1,500 r.p.m. Eight cylinders arranged V-type, water-cooled four-cycle, 4·7245-ins. bore by 5·1182-ins. stroke ; piston displacement, 718 cubic ins. Weight, including carburettor,

The rudder is hinged at a point about 10 ins. beyond the *fuselage* termination. The usual fixed stabilising plane and elevators are employed. The vertical fin extends 12 ins. forward of the leading edge of the tail plane.

magnetos, starting magneto, crank and propeller hub, but without radiator, water or oil, and without exhaust pipes, 445 lbs. Fuel consumption, ½ lb. of gas per horse-power hour ; oil consumption, 3 quarts per hour.—*Aerial Age, U.S.A.*

⊞ ⊞ ⊞ ⊞

The Homestead Association and Rest Homes.

AN appeal for assistance is being made by the above association, which aims at providing homesteads for discharged convalescent officers and men, where they may live and train after they have passed out of the range of medical treatment. The Association has already been presented with a small property " In Memoriam," and gifts may take the form of money, houses or land. Among the Vice-Presidents are Lieut.-General Sir David Henderson, K.C.B., Director-General of Military Aeronautics, and Lady Henderson, while Dr. C. Atkin Swan, who has done such splendid work in connection with the R.F.C. hospital, is the honorary medical consultant. Full particulars can be obtained from the Hon. Organising Secretary, Sergeant-Major D. Spencer, at 19–20, Craven Street, Strand, W.C. 2.

A flyer dated December 21, 1918. The war is clearly over—the Hispano-Suiza company is apparently now changing its market niche back to automobiles. During the First World War, when Georges Guynemer received his first Spad S.VII equipped with a Hispano-Suiza motor on August 27, 1916, he wrote to Louis Béchereau the next day praising the wonders of this new aeroplane. The air combat ace Guynemer thereafter had a long technical correspondence with Béchereau, whom he called the "ace of constructors" ("l'as des constructeurs"). It was Guynemer who later presented Béchereau with the medal of the *Chevalier* of the *Légion d'honneur* on July 12, 1917, in the SPAD works, in the presence of the minister of war. *Public domain*

Questions for Clay Hammond, vice president and chief pilot, regarding Old Rheinbeck Aerodrome's reproduction Spad VII, June 1, 2018

1. What are the best flight characteristics of the reproduction and what are the most problematic?

It has a thin airfoil on the wing. It has a very clean stall break, and it will experience accelerated stalls quite easily when angle of attack is exceeded. So we keep the speed up and avoid the hard pulls. Roll rate is great on ours. Having just gone through the rebuild and a full teardown inspection, we knew what we had in terms of structural integrity and strength when we put it all back together, so I was more comfortable with it than before in terms of trying some maneuvers that were more aerobatic in nature. I did a couple split-S maneuvers on the second test flight, and it would roll onto its back quickly for me to initiate the pull down to level flight again. The speed pays off quite abruptly as you start a climb, so I am hesitant to do a full loop with it. Maybe if we put a different prop on it that pulls a little better, I might try it.

2. Describe how best to turn a Spad VII.

Coordinated! Keep the ball centered / relative wind right on your nose . . . and watch it in the pull for it to stall. You'll feel the buffet, but it is quick and doesn't last long before it breaks out the rest of the way. . . . Found out the hard way in a turn once during the Sunday airshow dogfight.

3. Have you ever engaged in mock dogfighting maneuvers, and, if so, what were they?

I fly it in the dogfight at ORA on a regular basis, but we don't hold to Boelcke's Dicta in any way, shape, or form. I've done the tight turns though, and the split-S, and they are mentioned above. Pretty much any dogfight or aerobatic maneuver (interchangeable?) consists of a loop, roll or spin . . . or a combination of any of the three. I've done the half roll with it, and I think it is pretty good. Don't want to full loop it unless we can get some more climb power out of it. And I have no plans to ever spin it intentionally.

Two images of the Old Rhinebeck Aerodrome's reproduction Spad VII in George Turnure's colors, seen flying over the Rhinebeck area. ORA has weekend airshows May through October every weekend—if you've never been, the visit will be well worth the effort! *David Trost, Old Rhinebeck Aerodrome volunteer*

CHAPTER 4

Spad VII C.1 180 Horsepower

The Spad VII with the original 150 hp engine was still not competitive with German Albatros and Fokker aircraft. Birkigt redesigned the compression of his engine from 4:7:1 to 5:3:1 in the spring of 1917 (Kowalski 2007, 17). The result was the Hisso 180 hp engine (Hispano-Suiza 8Ab). The first to fly this more powerful Spad VII C.1 was Georges Guynemer (S254)—resulting in nineteen victories. The problem next became one of production— the SPAD company could not deliver in quantity. Thus began licensing of other companies to produce enough Spads to meet the demand. The following factories were licensed to produce Spads in France: Blériot Aéronautique, Les Ateliers d'Aviation L. Janoir, Kellner et ses Fils, Construction Aéronautique Edmond de Marçay, L'Atelier de Construction d'Apareils d'Aviation Roger Sommer, Les Ateliers de Construction Régy Frères, Société d'Études Aéronautiques (SEA), and Grémont. In Russia, the one factory that manufactured Spads was Duks Company in Moscow, and in England the two companies were Mann, Egerton & Co. in Norwich and L. Bleriot Ltd. in Brooklands (Kowalski 2007, 18).

The 180 hp engine provided enough extra power to increase the Spad rate of climb from 6 minutes 40 seconds to 4 minutes 40 seconds, and its speed at level flight from 112 mph (150 hp) to 127 mph (Guttman 2009, 24). The only downside was the carburetor, which was unreliable. The Spad VII with the 180 hp Hisso was said by Frank Tallman to be the sweetest of the Spad aircraft, and many pilots of the time felt the same way, since the Spad VII 180 hp was lighter, had a reasonably reliable engine with good power-to-weight ratio, and was more maneuverable than the bigger, heavier Spad XIII, which was prone to problems with its spur-geared 220 hp engine.

The Spad VII with the 180 hp engine. Note the side panels with louvers, indicating operation during cooler weather. Keeping the temperature of the engine at optimal levels required constant tweaking with the Hisso engines. Note also the camouflage by the tail feathers, and the extreme thinness of the wings at the tips. To enter the Spad cockpit, the pilot placed his right foot in the stirrup and his left foot atop a pad on the exhaust, finally swinging himself into the Spad cockpit. *NARA 18-WP-1650*

Visible in this image are the louvers inside the cowl opening—this was the final form of screening used in the Spad VII. Earlier models featured perforated panels that allowed different amounts of air to pass through given average temperatures produced by various seasons. The louvers were able to be manipulated (like a venetian blind) from the cockpit, allowing the pilots to precisely control the temperature of the engine. Also note the slight undercambering of the wings, and the French cockades on the underside of the bottom wing. *NARA 18-WP-1651*

In this image, the rib spacing of the wings is clearly visible—note how closely they are spaced together. The Spad airfoil was extremely thin which required higher speeds to achieve sufficient lift. Many of those transitioning from Nieuports to Spads experienced a learning curve adjusting to the higher speeds required to take off and land a Spad. Closely spacing the ribs provided the necessary strength to the wings. Also note the mesh screen in the cowl opening of this aircraft, which indicated an earlier model and warmer weather. *NARA 18-WP-12917*

Spad VIIs lined up on the flight line. The simple "S" painted on the rudder would become emblematic with all Spad aircraft, telling you in one letter who built the aircraft. Note the plumb trailing edge of the rudder, also indicating at a glance that this was a Spad VII and not a Spad XI, XIII, or XVI.
NARA 165-WW-22C-10

In this interesting image, a mechanic is seen tapping loose the metal propeller hub from the wooden propeller or visa versa, while an officer looks on. The pilot is in the cockpit, presumably waiting to test the new propeller. The propellers on Spads were around 8 feet in diameter, which kept high-pressured air flowing over the elevators and rudder, making them extra responsive. *Public domain*

Below and above: 1916 Spad VII, known as the "Cambrai" Spad, due to the fact that it was restored and placed on temporary display at the Musée de Cambrai, in France. The restoration effort was led by Philippe Mace, president of the Louis-Bleriot Association and grandson of the famous aviation pioneer Louis Bleriot. It features an original working Hisso engine. *Creative Commons Vassil*

The Spad VII featured a distinctive stabilizer, elevator, and rudder shape, making them easily distinguishable from the Spad XIII. The cockades painted on the horizontal stabilizer and elevators helped initially identify the Spads, since they were sometimes confused with German aircraft due to their lack of wing dihedral like the Albatros D. I and D. II, and nominally the Halberstadt D. II. *Public domain*

Another famous ace's Spad VII: Georges Guynemer's. Here is his Spad "Vieux Charles" (visible just under the exhaust stack) on a flatbed trailer, presumably after his death. The lower planes are lashed together on the right, and the upper plane is to the left. Guynemer's Spad VII is preserved for posterity in the French National Air & Space Museum (*Le Musée de l'Air et de l'Espace*) in Paris (see chapter 7).
Public domain, source: Université de Caen Normandie

One of the few remaining photographs showing George Guynemer in his Spad VII "Vieux Charles." Guynemer was instrumental in Spad design due to his close relationship with Louis Béchereau. Note the additional louvers in the check engine panels, indicating yet another iteration of how finicky the cooling of the Hisso was. Also note the parceled flying wires—actually two wires covered with linen and doped. This was also done on various other Allied aircraft.
Public domain

A British Egerton Mann Spad VII looking somewhat out of place on a paved tarmac. Note the screened apertures in the engine check panels—yet another variation of the cooling problem.
Bill Larkins

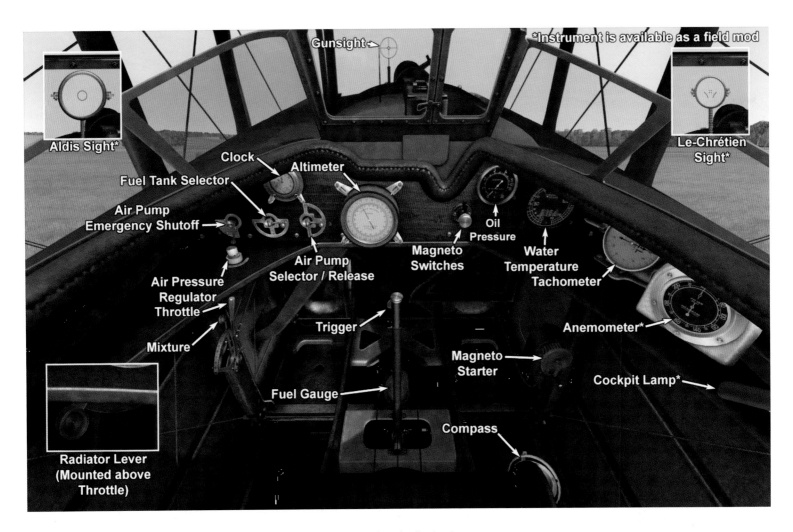

Gunsight →

*Instrument is available as a field mod

Aldis Sight*

Le-Chrétien Sight*

Clock

Altimeter

Fuel Tank Selector

Air Pump Emergency Shutoff →

Oil Pressure

Air Pump Selector / Release

Magneto Switches

Water Temperature Tachometer

Air Pressure Regulator Throttle →

Trigger

Mixture

Anemometer*

Magneto Starter

Fuel Gauge

Cockpit Lamp* →

Compass

Radiator Lever (Mounted above Throttle)

An illustration of the cockpit of the Spad VII 180 hp. Note that the return track and roller for the spent cartridge belt has been eliminated in favor of a simple "dump chute" that exits on the port side of the fuselage. Also note the radiator lever, which is mounted under the plywood apron on the port side—this indicates a late-model Spad VII 180 hp. *Courtesy Rise of Flight*

This image depicts a Spad VII that was captured by the Germans. The cheek covers have been removed, as has the starboard access panel near the rudder bar. There is a large flak hole near where the pilot was sitting, so perhaps he was wounded when he landed behind enemy lines. Also note that the upper engine access panel is torn and twisted, and the prop is broken. At the end of the exhaust stack, an unusual amount of soot is visible on the fuselage, indicating that this pilot most likely suffered engine troubles as well as being hit himself. *Greg VanWyngarden*

The Spad VII (1615) of *Lafayette Escadrille* pilot Harold Willis of SPA 124. During an escort patrol on August 18, 1917, fire from enemy fighters disabled his Spad—he dove the Spad, with enemy fighters following him down, continuing to fire. His engine was dead, so he made a daring and successful dead-stick landing on a hill overlooking Dun-sur-Meuse. His pursuers landed and *Leutnant* Wilhelm Schulz took him prisoner—later Willis would describe him as "a very decent fellow and good sport" (Steven A. Ruffin, The Lafayette Escadrille, Philadelphia: Casemate, 2016, p. 139). *Greg VanWyngarden*

In these two images, the captured Willis Spad 1615 is seen being repainted in German markings. It would become part of *Jasta 16b*. Capturing of enemy aircraft and repurposing them was done on both sides during the war.
Greg VanWyngarden

The following is stunt pilot Frank Tallman's commentary on flying the Spad VII 180 hp aircraft:

"Before flight, we had to set the Spad in level-flight position and fill the header tank first, then the radiator, to eliminate, as much as possible, the steam-provoking air bubbles. Once in a position for takeoff, I hauled my six-foot . . . frame over the exhaust pipe and dropped it into a small comfortable cockpit. . . . I turned the fuel-on switch off, and we went through the starting procedure that is necessary to start a Hisso. It includes checking if the fuel pump is operative. We also rock the propeller until fuel spills from the carburetor; then with contact, the pilot madly spins the booster coil and mechanic flips the prop backward. It kicks forward and catches, and the Hisso rumbles nicely as the pressure and temperature rise. With mechanics holding the wings, I check the mags at full throttle, but like the SE5, because of the long [exhaust] stacks, the engine is making about as much noise as a kitten with a stomachful of cream, and it just doesn't sound like enough commotion to fly the airplane. Pointing the Spad into the 15-knot wind . . . I pour the coal on. Instantly the tail is up, and I have complete rudder control. I am off the ground and climbing in about 150 feet. The push-pull ailerons are delightful, and the response is equal to or exceeds that of our present crop of aircraft.

A climb into the afternoon local traffic is at about 60 mph, with a wary eye evenly divided between traffic and a rising water temperature. I am aware that my head is about even with the top wing, and in case of an emergency and a rollover, I could get to be the original flat top! Because of the closely placed center section struts and the Vickers gun, the Spad is no Cessna 310 or Piper Aztec as far as visibility goes, so I leave the pattern for a session of fun and games. The Hisso idles beautifully, and power off stalls occur at 47 mph, with a positive and quick nose drop. . . . The Spad VII control travel is measured by the baker's dozen rule and exceeds anything the modern pilot is familiar with. This could be a boon in combat. . . . I enjoy large control throw, and the challenge of smooth, coordinated flight in the Spad is a real pleasure.

Climbing out with the Spad is a commando operation with one's nerves, watching water temperature rise and oil pressure fall. . . . Flying straight and level, I feel like the stilt man in the circus, because my eye level exactly splits the trailing edge of the center section, i.e., of the top wing. . . . The Spad VII's characteristics in the air, to me at least, most nearly resembles a Great Lakes BG-1 . . . they have a flight responsiveness that makes them, if not brothers, at least relatives.

With fly-through maneuvers like the loop, I start at 135 mph, and halfway up I can either quit or go through with ball-bearing facility. It goes over nicely, but you see the flying wires slightly bowing all the way around. . . . I . . . try to stay within 2 to 2.5 Gs in maneuvers with the old girls. Slow rolls are a combination of slow roll and aileron roll and come through nicely at 110 mph without enough altitude loss to upset the most stringent FAA flight examiner.

Cuban 8s are a combination of the above, but aerobatics with the Spad are always leavened by a hawklike view of the water temperature gauge, which can change [rapidly]. A speed of 55 to 65 mph was adequate for the approach, and I touched wheels first on the concrete at about 48 mph. Holding the tail up with just enough power, I rolled onto the grass, immediately sucking the stick back and digging in the tail skid. With blasts from the Hisso over the rudder to keep the course straight, I stopped in about 250 feet."

Tallman continues by describing the Spad VII used in a World War I documentary film: "In limited combat I found the Spad noticeably more maneuverable than the S.E.5, better than the Pfalz DXII, and better in some respects than the Camel or Nieuport. It is, of course, more limber than anything except the Camel, and with the exclusion of the rust-throwing radiator and heater, the engine pure reliability, and I would trust it as I do the Continentals in my Cessna 310."

CHAPTER 5
The Spad XI, XII, and XVI

The Spad XI C.2 represented an effort to design a two-seater Spad, partly on the basis of the success of the Spad VII C.1 and partly in an effort to find a replacement for the aging Sopwith 1½ Strutter. The performance of the XI C.2 was poor—it was tail heavy, making it hard on the pilot, and also it showed a tendency to stall. It was also underpowered, since it had the same Hispano-Suiza 180 hp engine that the Spad VIIs did; some were replaced with twelve-cylinder Renault engines, but this only made its performance worse! In spite of this, around 1,000 were built and twelve squadrons were equipped with them, but they all were retired by the fall of 1918, having been replaced with the nominally better Spad XVI.

The Spad XII C.A.1 was the brainchild of Georges Guynemer, who approached Louis Béchereau about fitting a Hotchkiss cannon to be fired through the propeller shaft of a geared 200 hp Hisso—the first mention of this aircraft was in December 1916. The XII

was similar in appearance to the early-production Spad XIII, although the XI, XII, and XVI all had swept wings. It was heavier (by 407 lbs.) and larger than the Spad VII and was difficult to fly by any but the most-experienced pilots. In addition to the 37 mm cannon and rounds for twelve shots, it had a Vickers gun mounted offset to starboard; the cockpit filled with smoke from the cannon, impairing visibility and adding to the awkwardness of fighting in this machine.

The Spad XVI was essentially the Spad XI with a Lorraine-Dietrich engine of between 240 and 250 hp, which made the XVI heavier and more powerful, but it still suffered from poor handling qualities. The Spad XVI arrived at the front in late 1917 to early 1918 and equipped thirty-two French *escadrilles*. In total, 305 two-seater Spads, comprising mostly Spad XVIs, were operational with French reconnaissance *escadrilles* at the Armistice (as compared to 530 Salmson and 645 Breguet reconnaissance aircraft).

Although much larger and relatively unsuccessful, the Spad XI bears similarities to the highly successful Spad line of fighters. It has similar landing gear, fuselage, and tail feathers, but unlike the fighters, it has swept wings and four sets of interplane struts that are not parallel but are canted inward as they move from the lower planes to the upper planes. Presumably these attachment points line up on the main spars for each wing. The wider placement on the lower wings most likely is to provide greater support to the lower wing and prevent wing flutter. *Air Service, United States Army, public domain*

SPAD S.XI at Air Service Production Center No. 2, Romorantin Aerodrome, France, 1918. A view from astern—note the horizontal stabilizer is very similar to the Spad XIII. The ailerons resemble the Spad VII's, and note the twin Lewis guns mounted on a traversable gun ring. The XI was a bit tail heavy, and most likely the gun position had something to do with this. *Air Service, United States Army, public domain*

Spad XIs of *Escadrille* 34 lined up
on the flight line ready for action,
and another image shows them in
a radial deployment off the flight
line. Note the distinctive fox icon
on the fuselage in the final image.
Greg VanWyngarden

Spad XI from *Escadrille* 42. In the first image it appears as though the gunner is handing off either an exposed roll of film, or being handed a fresh roll. The engine is still running and the wheels are not chocked—the pilot is looking on with a grin. In the second image the use of the rear gun is demonstrated by the gunner. *Greg VanWyngarden*

In this drawing, the Spad XI seems to be a stretched version of the XIII in profile, except note the amount of stagger of the two wings—the Spad fighters had no such stagger. The XI also retains the pushrod and bell crank aileron actuation assembly as in the fighters. This is a good example of how the right proportion of features can contribute to a successful aircraft, but when enlarged or modified excessively the secret recipe is lost!
Flight magazine

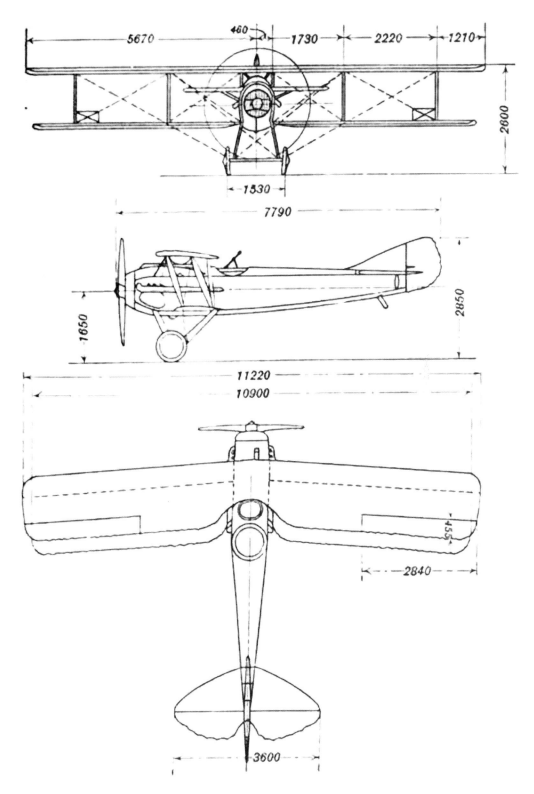

The Spad two-seater S. XI, 200 h.p. Hispano-Suiza engine.

This fascinating drawing from *Flight* magazine shows measured drawings of the Spad airfoil, which is similar in shape to all the Spad aircraft. It also contains materials used for major structural components, as well as a diagram illustrating how the ailerons were actuated by using the pushrods and bell cranks contained in the lower wing. It is interesting that the same 200 hp Hispano-Suiza was used to power the Spad XIII and the Spad XI—the latter being a larger, heavier aircraft.

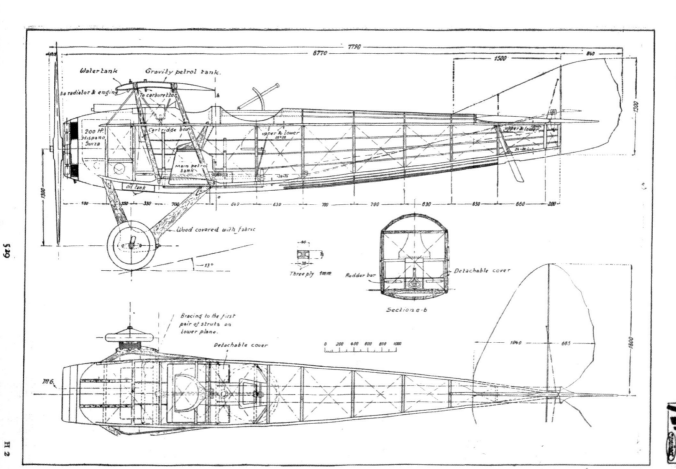

May 16, 1918.

The Spad two-seater S. XI, 200 h.p. Hispano-Suiza engine.

In this plan and elevation drawing of the Spad XI—also from *Flight* magazine—the major structural aspects of the fuselage are illustrated, including longerons, struts, bracing wires, and the layout of the cabane struts and their supports between the longerons. The run of the elevator and rudder cables is also drawn. The pilot's seat rests on the main fuel tank, which is something that may have caused some anxiety in combat. The upper wing contained the header fuel tank as well as a water tank used to cool the engine—both were gravity feed.

A Spad XII of the 13th Aero Squadron, 2nd Pursuit Group, belonging to Capt. Charles J. Biddle. "The Devil's Own Grim Reapers" (squadron nickname) were charged with protecting the St. Mihiel sector and were successful in attacking and destroying many enemy aircraft and balloons. The Spad XII carried a 37 mm Puteaux cannon that fired through the crankshaft of the engine. The shells had to be loaded and unloaded by hand, making combat flying while doing this problematic due to propellant fumes filling the cockpit after each shot. Aces such as Guynemer and Fonck fought in the Spad XII with some success. *Air Service, United States Army, public domain*

Clamped to the fuselage framing of the Golden Age Air Museum's Spad XIII replica is a mockup of the 13th Aero's squadron insignia, which was copied from the original artifact that was removed from Biddle's Spad by his mechanic. It is likely this project will be nearing completion sometime in 2020. *GAAM*

A candid view of a mechanic or another pilot, looking back at the photographer in the Spad XII pictured opposite. The Spad XII had a slight positive stagger to the wings—much less than in the Spad XI but still noticeable. Note the absence of the blister fairings for the valve covers of the engine, so prevalent in other Spads. Biddle was entrusted with the only Spad XII given to the Americans by the French. *Air Service, United States Army, public domain*

The unique Hispano-Suiza-geared 220 hp 8Cb engine. The gearing allowed the 37 mm cannon to pass through the hub of the propeller, and this engine had a clockwise-turning propeller as opposed to the more typical counterclockwise turn of other Hisso engines. In addition to discharge fumes, the breech of the cannon interfered with the normal operation of the stick, forcing an awkward split setup similar to that used by Deperdussin. *Duch.seb Creative Commons Attribution—Share Alike 3.0 Unported, 2.5 Generic, 2.0 Generic, and 1.0 Generic license*

Spad XII 400 at Velizy-Villacoublay aerodrome on September 7, 1918, and Spad XII 440, also at Villacoublay. *Greg VanWyngarden*

The Spad XVI was an improved version of the Spad XI, essentially with a more powerful engine resulting in a heavier aircraft that was inferior to the plane it was meant to improve on! The Spad XVIs arrived at the front in late 1917 and equipped twenty-seven French squadrons. The Spad XVI pictured here is at the Chief of Air Service Headquarters, American Expeditionary Forces (AEF), and is Gen. William "Billy" Mitchell's personal aircraft. *Air Service, United States Army, public domain*

Another view of Mitchell's Spad XVI in France. The French gave six Spad XVIs to the AEF in August 1918. The one pictured here, serial number 9392, became Mitchell's personal aircraft. Mitchell's Spad XVI was transferred to the Smithsonian Institution in 1920. *Air Service, United States Army, public domain*

Spad XVIs from *Escadrille* 225 lined up on the flight line. *Greg VanWyngarden*

Pilot and gunner of a Spad XVI look semiapprovingly at the photographer. *Greg VanWyngarden*

Mitchell used his Spad XVI to perform reconnaissance patrols during the last few months of the war. In this image, a Spad XVI (not Mitchell's) is seen on patrol in the Compiègne sector in this rare image. Note the horse-drawn wagons on the road below, which are in focus, and the somewhat blurred Spad—obviously the photographer was more concerned with what was occurring on the ground than in the air! *NASM-SI-75-12263*

Mitchell's fully restored Spad XVI as seen today at the Udvar-Hazy Center of the National Air & Space Museum in Chantilly, Virginia. Note the large fairings on the cowling that conceal the engine. Also note the many bandings on the spruce interplane struts—this was done to compress the wood fibers and prevent them from splitting under load. *Cliff, Creative Commons Attribution 2.0 Generic license*

A view of the same aircraft from above—note the pronounced sweep of the wings, and the elongated horizontal stabilizer/elevator (relative to a Spad XIII). Also note the nose webs at the leading edge between each rib. This was done to preserve the shape of the leading edge of the airfoil, to make it more efficient at high speeds. *Cliff, Creative Commons Attribution 2.0 Generic license*

CHAPTER 6
The Spad XIII C.1

The Spad XIII was largely a response to the fact that the earlier Spads had only one machine gun—most German fighters, such as the Albatros D. III, DV, DVa, and Pfalz D.IIIs, featured dual Spandau machine guns, so the XIII featured dual .303 Vickers guns with 400 rounds apiece. In addition, an increase in speed and rate of climb made the Spad XIII a formidable adversary, and it first flew on April 4, 1917. At its core was a Hispano-Suiza 200 hp 8Ba geared engine developed by Marc Birkigt (later models reached between 220 and 235 hp). The gearing was problematic and was not fully resolved before the war ended. The average lifespan of a geared Hisso was around 15–20 missions before needing replacement. Also, with a larger engine and an extra machine gun, the airframe was beefed up a bit to compensate for the added weight and stress. The XIII also featured a different empennage shape and slightly enlarged ailerons to give the roll rate slightly more punch. The windscreen was reconfigured, and more instruments were added to monitor the larger engine. In spite of the increased speed, rate of climb, and firepower, many pilots still preferred the Spad VII, with the 180 hp engine, sacrificing the attributes of the XIII for increased maneuverability. Nonetheless, by the end of 1918, 8,472 had been built by Spad and eight other companies under license. Spad XIIIs were flown by American, British, French, Italian, Belgian, and Russian squadrons.

Specifications for the Spad XIII C.1	
Crew	1
Propulsion	1 piston engine
Engine	Model Hispano-Suiza 8Ba–c
Engine power	200–220 hp
Top speed (level flight)	135.5 mph at 6,560 ft.
Service ceiling	21,818–22,360 ft.
Range	171 miles
Empty weight	1,245 lbs.
Gross	1,808 lbs.
Wingspan	26 ft. 11 in.
Wing area	227 ft.²
Length	20 ft. 8 in.
Height	7 ft. 11 in.
First flight	April 4, 1917
Total production	8,472

Dimensions taken from NASM Spad XIII, Smith IV.

Rounded wingtips were characteristic of the early Spad XIIIs. When the change came to squared-off tips, "pockets" were fitted over the aft portion of the rounded tips to make them square. In this image it is clearly colder weather, as evidenced by the closed louvers at the cowl opening, louvered solid cheek panels, and overcoats worn by the men standing around the aircraft. The chocks are off the wheels, indicating that this Spad XIII has either just landed or is preparing for takeoff; due to the closed louvers, it seems more likely the latter. *NARA 165-WW-21B-27*

Another early Spad (note the rounded wingtips) that has suffered a complete collapse of its landing gear. The circumstances of the accident are unknown; however, many pilots transitioning from Nieuports to Spads were unaccustomed to the higher speeds required for takeoffs and landings. This pilot may have overrun the landing strip and encountered rougher terrain, which may have caused the landing gear to fail, or he may have reduced throttle too soon, causing the thin airfoil to become ineffective—thus dropping the plane heavily onto the ground (stall). *NARA 165-WW-1A-26*

Clockwise from upper left corner:

An image of another early Spad XIII with rounded wing tips.

A view showing the aft end of the twin Vickers .303 machine guns and how the breech affects the cockpit. Also visible is the redesigned windscreen—much smaller than the wraparound windshield characteristic of the Spad VIIs.

The business end of the twin Vickers, showing how they carefully fit over the engine and straddle the intake manifolds and header tank plumbing. Also visible are the ammo feed/dump shoots and ammunition magazines.

The same picture now completely cowled in. The forward visibility of the Spad aircraft was less than the Nieuports, but they had speed, ruggedness, and, with the XIII, firepower.

Another aft view of the Vickers guns and cockpit. Note the dual triggers on the stick, and the troughs in the cowling to accommodate the cocking arms. Forward of the grillwork, the all-important radiator is visible.

A side elevation on the starboard side, showing a wealth of information: the raked cabane struts are characteristic of the Spad XIII; the forward bracing wire is faired with wood, so it resembles a strut but is really a fairing. The lower wing root attachment points and corresponding attachment points for the main gear are also visible, as is the starboard cylinder head cover. Note in the lower portion of the cockpit the oil line running to the aft portion of the engine. *NARA 18-WP-56471-W*

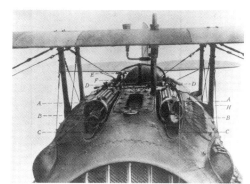

A Spad XIII preparing for takeoff. Note the spoked wheels, which have no covers fitted, and the banded landing-gear struts. Banding was done by using thin line wrapped tightly around the struts, to compress the wood fibers of the spruce struts to prevent them from splitting under load. *Library of Congress 10531*

Lt. Georges Charles Marie Francois Flachaire stands nonchalantly next to his Spad XIII (previous image depicted him taking off). *Library of Congress 10530*

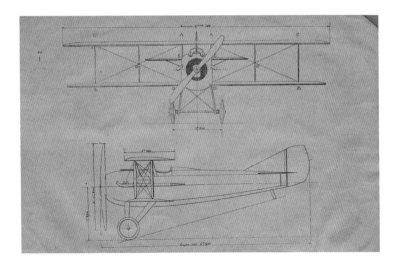

Excerpts and cover of a French Spad XIII manual that describes basic proportions of the Spad XIII. The manual also includes assembly and engine use instructions, as well as tips for the various quirks of the Spad XIII regarding fuel systems and keeping the engine temperature at the correct level in various climates. *Mike O'Neal*

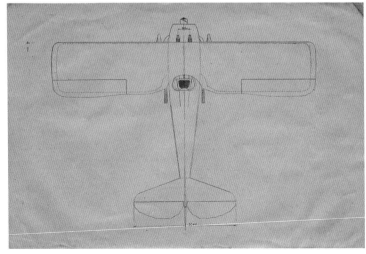

This image depicts the massive Spad propeller—close to 9 feet in diameter. Also note the covered wheels (no spokes showing), and twin Vickers machine guns. The twin guns gave the Spad XIII parity with German fighters, which with the advent of the Albatros line of fighters had twin Spandau machine guns as standard equipment. *NARA 165-WW-15D-14*

An Italian Spad XIII that has come to grief inverted. The landing-gear axles appear to be bent—indicating a hard landing—although the strut system appears intact. Also note that the wing structure appears intact as well—a testament to the ruggedness of the Spad aircraft. It is difficult to say what may have caused this accident, although the rough terrain and underbrush may indicate a forced landing or overshooting of the primary runway. *Österreichische Nationalbibliothek (Austrian National Library), public domain*

A Spad XIII at Camp Rathbun in Desoronto, Canada, in 1918, most likely in the spring. This camp was set up by the Royal Flying Corps to train pilots—nearly 1,300 were trained here. Pilots were trained mostly on Jennies (Cannucks), which makes this an unusual image showing a Spad with machine guns removed. Note the car filled with tourists in the background—watching the flight training at this camp was a popular form of entertainment for the people who lived near Camp Rathbun. *Desoronto Archives*

A Spad XIII used for a Fourth of July parade. It is festooned with American flags and bunting and is fascinating in that the slow billowing of the flags is captured in the image—hence the blurring. The Spad XIII became the primary mount for American pilots after the Nieuport 28. In the US the Spad XIII became synonymous with the success of Eddie Rickenbacker—Medal of Honor recipient and America's "Ace of Aces." Note the tail skid cart, and the absence of the exhaust stacks on the fuselage.
NARA 18-WP-18401

This Spad XIII belonged to the 22nd Aero Squadron. This image was taken after the Armistice, as the squadron insignia was not applied to aircraft until after the war. Note that one of the engine access panels has been removed on the forward portion of the cowling, indicating that engine servicing was being performed when this photo was taken. *NARA 18-WP-207385*

This postwar Spad XIII was part of the fledgling Imperial Japanese Army Air Service. The French Aeronautical Mission was the first foreign military mission to Japan since the 1890s and was sent in 1918 to help Japan develop an air force. The mission was led by Jacques-Paul Faure and comprised sixty-three members, who brought with them Salmson, Nieuport, Spad XIII, and Breguet XIV aircraft, as well as Caquot dirigibles. Note in this photograph the plumed officer instructing the pilots in a group to the right. Also note that these Spads were most likely used for reconnaissance, since they lack armament and have camera equipment installed on the port side (as evidenced by the "photo" painted on the starboard side). *Kitagawa shashinkan, public domain*

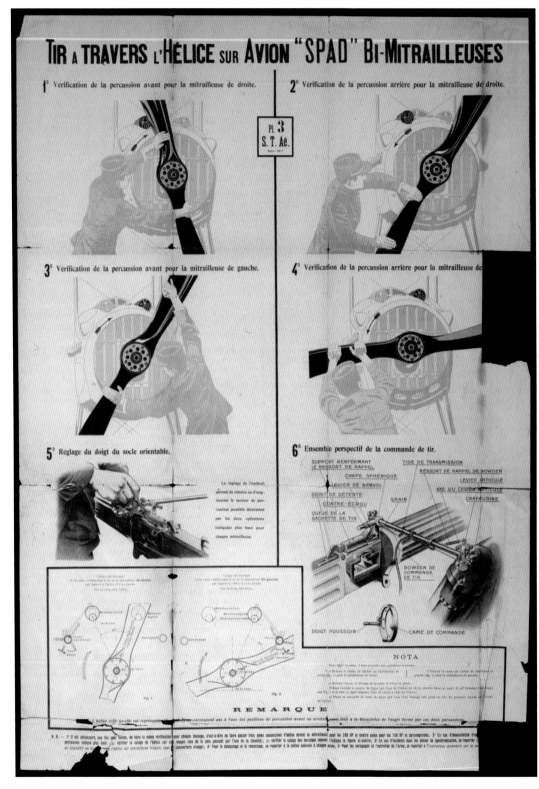

This poster illustrates the proper method for aligning the Spad interrupter gear that enabled the twin Vickers machine guns to fire between the propeller blades. Early attempts before the interrupter gear were semidisastrous, since a pilot could conceivably shoot off his propeller! *NASM*

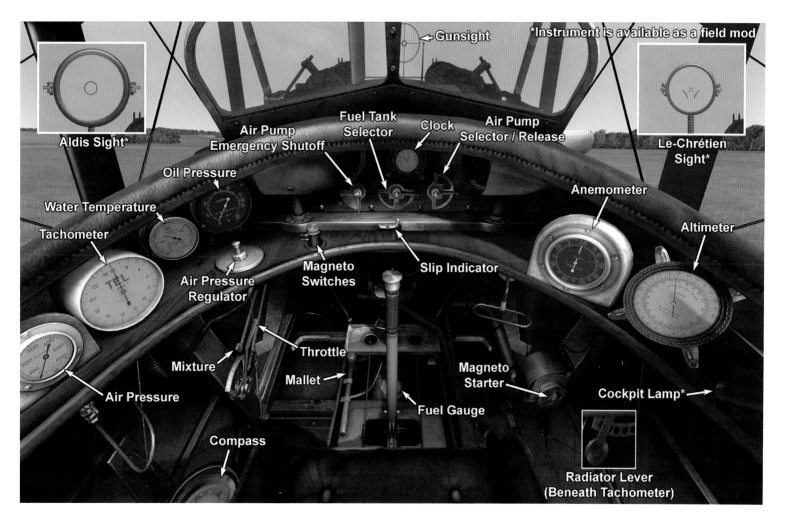

Gunsight

*Instrument is available as a field mod

Aldis Sight*

Le-Chrétien Sight*

Air Pump Emergency Shutoff

Fuel Tank Selector

Clock

Air Pump Selector / Release

Oil Pressure

Anemometer

Water Temperature

Altimeter

Tachometer

Air Pressure Regulator

Magneto Switches

Slip Indicator

Throttle

Mixture

Mallet

Magneto Starter

Cockpit Lamp*

Air Pressure

Fuel Gauge

Compass

Radiator Lever (Beneath Tachometer)

This illustration graphically depicts the instrument and control layout of the Spad XIII. The instrumentation is more complete in the XIII than the Spad VII and includes numerous new engine instruments to monitor the geared 220 hp Hispano-Suiza. Instruments on the plywood apron that surround the pilot have the feel of so many curios arranged on a table. *Image courtesy of Rise of Flight*

An interesting postwar image of many aircraft, trucks, wagons, and Spads and Spad parts scattered like so much rubbish on a road at the First Air Depot at Columbry-les-Belles. Before the squadron departed for home, engines were removed from the aircraft for reuse, and the remaining airframes and other material were readied to be set afire! This was done all over France as war-weary soldiers wanted to put the war—and any reminder of it—behind them. *NARA 165-WW-279B-004*

A close-up of the nose of a captured Spad XIII—note the German with his hand draped over the aft landing wire in the background of the image. This picture shows the top of the Hispano-Suiza 200 hp engine and how the twin Vickers machine guns were carefully fitted around in the intake manifolds of the engine. Also note the louvers in the cowl opening and the honeycombing of the radiator face. *Greg VanWyngarden*

CHAPTER 7
Spad Aces and the Opposition

The Spad VII and XIII remained in service until the end of the war and, in the right hands, were formidable fighting machines—capable of diving away from trouble at speeds few German planes could match (with the exception of the Fokker D.VIIF). Those pilots who excelled with the Spad were extremely aware of what it could do and could not do—it was not a turn fighter, instead relying on its speed, ruggedness, and firepower to shoot down the enemy. The Spad was the mount for many of the top aces in the French air force, and there were some notable aces in the British, American, and Italian air forces. There were not as many British Spad aces due to the fact that the RFC mandated use of the S.E.5a aircraft by around mid-1917. However, Spad VIIs were used by the RFC until the S.E.5a arrived—the British solution to the Hisso engine.

Tactics varied among Spad aces, but all used speed and the power dive to advantage. Guynemer and Fonck would attack out of the sun, diving at high speed toward an unsuspecting foe, and would "put my bullets into the target as if I placed them there by hand," as Fonck was fond of saying. The fatal blow having been delivered, the Spad ace would recover from the power dive and then zoom back up to repeat the maneuver if needed. Raoul Lufbery of the *Lafayette Escadrille* would dive his Spad under an enemy aircraft, zoom up, and—when close—fire into the belly of his opponent, executing a stall turn and then diving away to pick up speed again. Those who tried to fly the Spad like a Nieuport, Hanriot, Sopwith, or other turn fighters were lucky if they survived the engagement to tell the tale.

Georges Guynemer has become as synonymous with the Spad as Rene Fonck—two of France's top-scoring aces. As mentioned earlier, Guynemer was responsible for many of the improvements to the Spad fighter, due to his long-standing correspondence with Louis Béchereau. In this portrait of Guynemer, his bemused gaze belies his thoughts. *Library of Congress 21149*

Georges Guynemer stands with Capt. Antonin Brocard—Guynemer's commanding officer. Brocard commanded such aces as Guynemer, Fonck, Heurteaux, Dorme, Garros, Vedrines, Deullin, and De La Tour. On July 3, 1915, Brocard scored the first victory for the squadron, N.3, while flying a single-seater conversion Nieuport X. He shot down a German Albatros near Napier-Compiegne with his rifle! Guynemer assisted Brocard with this victory. On October 25, 1916, Brocard was placed in command of the "Storks" (*Groupe des Cigognes*) group of squadrons, which was composed of N.3, N.103, N.26, and N.73. *Le Journal le Miroir*

Guynemer's Spad XII photographed at St. Pol. Note the ever-present "Vieux Charles," which was painted on all of Guynemer's Spads. A friendly dog is seen greeting the photographer in the one image, and it is lying in repose in the shade of the aircraft in the other photo. In the image below, an armature can be seen mounted to the far set of cabane struts just in front of the windscreen. This was used to mount a camera that Guynemer used to take images of his victims, to prove he shot them down. *Greg VanWyngarden*

One of the few photos in existence of Guynemer in the cockpit of his Spad VII, "Vieux Charles." On October 10, 1915, Guynemer was assigned a Nieuport X (no. 320) that had belonged to Sgt. Armand Bonnard, who had named it "Vieux Charles"—perhaps in homage to the oldest pilot of the squadron— Charles Jules Vedrines; Guynemer kept the name and used it on all his subsequent aircraft for luck. Note the strong early-morning light and "Storks" insignia on the fuselage. Image was taken by Robert Soubiron, who would join the famed *Lafayette Escadrille. Library of Congress 5310*

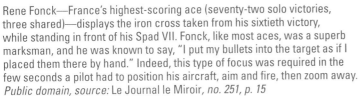

Rene Fonck—France's highest-scoring ace (seventy-two solo victories, three shared)—displays the iron cross taken from his sixtieth victory, while standing in front of his Spad VII. Fonck, like most aces, was a superb marksman, and he was known to say, "I put my bullets into the target as if I placed them there by hand." Indeed, this type of focus was required in the few seconds a pilot had to position his aircraft, aim and fire, then zoom away. *Public domain, source:* Le Journal le Miroir, *no. 251, p. 15*

Portrait of Fonck taken in 1918. His chest is ablaze with medals of every kind—the Legion of Honor, *Croix de Guerre*, *Medaille Militaire*, Military Cross, Military Medal, and the Belgian *Croix de Guerre*. Fonck took great pride in his uniform and appearance—often spending his evenings ironing his clothes and poring over mission plans. He was uncomfortable around fellow pilots, however, tending toward bragging due to his social awkwardness. Consequently, many pilots avoided him! *Public domain, Bibliothèque Nationale de France*

Another image of Rene Fonck on a steamer ship. *Library of Congress 38713*

Charles Nungesser was the archetypal ace—he liked women, wine, and fast cars. He was wild at times and hated authority, such that he was placed under house arrest on occasion. He often would show up for a mission in his tuxedo and tails after carousing all night long. He'd hand his girlfriend whom he'd been partying with his tux coat and then put on his flying jacket, helmet, and gloves, and off he'd go on a dawn patrol. Nungesser didn't smile for photographs too much—all his front teeth were gone due to numerous crashes; instead, he sported a dazzling though unsettling smile of replacement gold teeth. This picture, taken in 1916, depicts a young Nungesser, whose piercing gaze is leveled at the photographer. *Public domain, Bibliothèque Nationale de France*

Before settling on the Spad XIII, Fonck also flew the Spad XII pictured here, which featured a 37 mm cannon whose bullets passed through the crankshaft of the motor. The shells were hand loaded into the breach by the pilot. In spite of these guns discharging large amount of smoke into the pilot's face, Fonck was able to shoot down eleven aircraft by using the cannon in the Spad XII. These aircraft took expert pilots to operate and, as a result, were replaced by the Spad XIII, which was easier for the pilot to fly while he was fighting. Here, Fonck is standing next to his Spad XIII. *Greg VanWyngarden*

In these two images, Capt. de Sevin, commander of SPA 26, climbs into Fonck's Spad XII S445 and is instructed by Fonck on how to best fly and fire the 37 mm cannon. Photo was taken at the aerodrome at Villeneuve-sur-Verberie in April 1918.
Greg VanWyngarden

Nungesser is seen standing in front of his Nieuport, featuring his signature logo—a black heart with the skull and crossed bones, coffin, and candles—which was painted on all of his aircraft, including his Spad XIII. The saying went "With a black heart, neither death nor the devil will prevail." Nungesser survived the war with forty-three victories and attempted to fly the Atlantic shortly before Charles Lindbergh in 1927. His plane "L'Oiseau Blanc" also sported this emblem when his luck ran out—some think he and Coli crashed in northern Maine or Nova Scotia. *NASM A-48746-A. public domain*

A portrait of Nungesser taken near the end of the war—note the quantity of medals on his tunic as compared with the previous photograph! Nungesser sustained perhaps more injuries than any other pilot, including a skull fracture, a brain concussion, multiple internal injuries, five fractures of the upper jaw, two fractures of his lower jaw, pieces of antiaircraft shrapnel embedded in his right arm, dislocation of both knees, redislocation of his left knee, bullet wounds in his mouth and in his ear, atrophy of tendons in his left leg, atrophy of muscles in his calf, a dislocated clavicle, a dislocated wrist, a dislocated right ankle, the loss of teeth, and miscellaneous contusions too numerous to mention. *Public domain, source: Marcel Jullian, Le chevalier du ciel: Un bagarreur héroïque; Charles Nungesser (Paris, Amiot-Dumont, 1953), p. 200*

Nungesser's Spad XII at Le Bourget field outside Paris. Nungesser sits in the cockpit, wearing his cap (not his aviator cap and goggles), as one mechanic appears ready to swing the prop. The wheels are chocked and clothing appears on the wingtip, so perhaps they are testing the engine or have finished performing routine maintenance. *Grey VanWyngarden*

America's Ace of Aces—Edward Vernon "Eddie" Rickenbacker, whose name was originally Rickenbacher; he replaced the "h" with a "k" to take the "Hun" out of his name. Capt. Eddie flew over 300 hours—more than any other American pilot—and shot down twenty-six planes. In this image he poses next to his Spad XIII of the 94th Aero ("Hat in the Ring") squadron. Rickenbacker knew how to fly the Spad XIII to advantage and by the end of the war had come to the conclusion that air combat was "scientific murder," such were the tactics by this time so codified and formulaic. *US Air Force Museum*

Another iconic image of Rickenbacker sitting in the cockpit of his Spad XIII—his steady appraising gaze resting on the photographer as if determining whether friend or foe. Rickenbacker survived the war and went on to fly in World War II and founded Eastern Airlines. He was awarded the Medal of Honor in 1931 by President Herbert Hoover for a dogfight in which he shot down two Fokker D. VIIs on the same day. *NARA ARC identifier: 530773, USAF museum*

An image of a German Han C.L. III A 3802 shot down by Eddie Rickenbacker and Lt. Reed Chambers, 94th Aero Squadron, on October 2, 1918—which is painted on the side of the fuselage, along with the 94th Aero's insignia. *Library of Congress 29542*

In this illustration, two Spad XIIIs are seen attacking what appears to be a very unfortunate Pfalz D. III. Although crude, it does illustrate the tactics of "boom and zoom" employed so effectively by Spad pilots. From an advantageous position above, Spads would attack at tremendous speed—firing within a window of just a few seconds before zooming back up to altitude. The poor Pfalz pilot probably never knew what hit him. Spads were not "turn fighters," so using their strengths (speed, which was extreme in a dive, and firepower) to advantage was the key to success. *Air Service, United States Army, public domain*

Lt. Frank Luke Jr. flew and fought with the 1st Pursuit Squadron. He was credited with eighteen victories and was known for his "balloon-busting" prowess. He is pictured in this image standing in front of his Spad XIII. Eddie Rickenbacker noted that "He was the most daring aviator and greatest fighter pilot of the entire war. His life is one of the brightest glories of our Air Service. He went on a rampage and shot down fourteen enemy aircraft, including ten balloons, in eight days. No other ace, even the dreaded Richthofen, had ever come close to that." *Public domain*

Luke standing in front of his thirteenth victory, an LVG C.V downed by Luke on September 18, 1918 at Rattentout. Luke was killed just eleven days later after shooting down two final balloons in the proximity of Dun-sur-Meuse, which was behind enemy lines. He was shot through the shoulder from ground fire, landing near Murveaux. He collapsed 200 meters from his plane as German troops were approaching. He was awarded the Medal of Honor posthumously in 1919, plus two Distinguished Service Cross citations (also posthumously). *NARA 111-SC-23128, 530751*

Count Francesco Baracca was Italy's premier ace, credited with thirty-four victories. Flying Nieuports originally, Baracca began flying Spad VIIs by March 1917. He preferred the Spad VII over the Spad XIII, although he liked the twin Vickers of the latter and tended to bounce between the two types. He commented that "It doesn't matter if the VII is equipped with a single gun. Provided you are a good fighter, a single gun is just enough." In this image Baracca is standing in front of his Spad XII—the same type flown by Guynemer and Fonck, which featured the 37 mm cannon that fired through the propeller hub. Also visible in this image is his personal logo—a black rearing stallion—paying tribute to his former cavalry unit, resulting in the sometime moniker of the "Cavalier of the Skies." Ferrari automobiles would adopt this icon for their cars after the war. Baracca failed to return from a strafing mission on June 19, 1918, near the Montello hill area. The charred remains of his Spad VII were found near Nervesa della Battaglia, where eventually a monument was built to memorialize the fallen aviator. *Public domain*

Raoul G. Lufbery was greatest ace from the famed *Lafayette Escadrille*—his official score was either 16 or 17 victories (accounts vary), but those who flew and fought with him stated that it was more like seventy or more. "Luf" is seen standing in front of his Spad VII, casually smoking a cigarette as the photographer took this picture. Many a pilot has stated that he owed his life to Lufbery, since the ace would fly top cover and keep an eye on new pilots. Lufbery was an inscrutable loner, and those who were his closest friends have commented that they didn't really know him. The French saw him as an American, but he saw himself as a Frenchman! Although born in Wallingford, Connecticut, he spent many formative years in France and cherished French culture and cooking—spending spare time between missions hunting for mushrooms in the forests surrounding his aerodrome. *Library of Congress 01970*

A replica of Luke's Spad XIII now adorns the Sky Harbor Airport in his hometown of Phoenix, Arizona. The plane is a composite of original parts from several aircraft (about 80 percent). It is on display in Terminal 3 of the airport. Luke's nickname was the "Arizona Balloon Buster." *Public domain image attribution: Marine 69-71 at en.wikipedia*

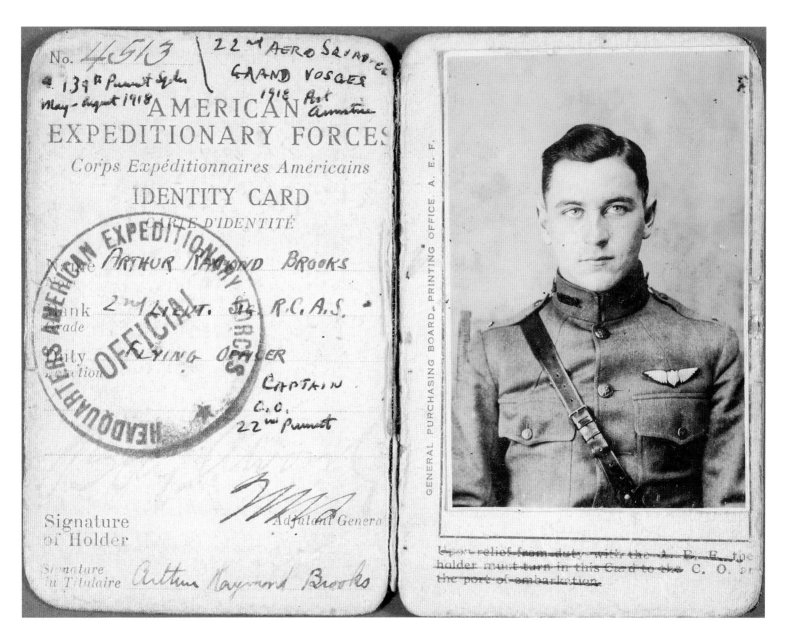

Second Lt. Arthur Raymond Brooks flew with the 22nd Aero Squadron and is perhaps best remembered for his solo dogfight against eight Fokker D. VII aircraft on September 14, 1918. During the dogfight, he shot down four of the D. VIIs, although he was officially credited with only two. The image depicts his identification card and includes some reference to his time training at the School of Military Aeronautics with the Royal Canadian Air Service (RCAS) from September to November 1917.
Public domain, US Army Air Service

In this image A. R. Brooks is seen standing in front of Spad XIII 18815, most likely in Colombey-les-Belles, France. This Spad XIII was flown mostly by commanding officer Capt. Ray C. Bridgman, but Brooks flew it on October 9, 1918, when he scored his sixth kill against a DFW (a German two-seater). Brooks eventually replaced Bridgman as CO of the 22nd, thus inheriting S18815. Brooks is probably most identified, however, with his "Smith" series of Spads (see chapter 8). *Public domain, Arthur Raymond Brooks Collection, Acc. 1989-0104, National Air & Space Museum, Smithsonian Institution*

A postwar Fokker D. VII—the foe that most Spad aces dreaded! The Fokker D. VII was designed by Anthony Fokker and Rhinehold Platz, and most historians agree that it was around sixteen years ahead of its time. It was designed to be easy to fly, since hastily trained pilots were rushed to frontline squadrons in a futile attempt to stem the Allied advance. The D. VII could hang on its propeller and fire into the belly of its opponent, and by the time the D. VIIF was introduced, it could match a Spad XIII in a dive. In this image, the Fokker D. VII is doing a loop! *Library of Congress*

Another image of a Fokker D. VII, taken during winter somewhere on the Western Front after the war. At the conclusion of the war, Germany was strictly forbidden from building any more of this airplane and had to hand over all parts, templates, and plans—such was its efficacy as a fighter plane. This was stipulated in the Treaty of Versailles. *State Archives of North Carolina ID 29840403806, original title WWI 55.B1.F15.6*

CHAPTER 8
Spads in Museums

Fortunately for World War I aviation enthusiasts, many original Spads exist in the permanent collections of various museums in the United States and abroad. Some are in near-original condition, such as Georges Guynemer's Spad VII, nicknamed "Vieux Charles," on display at La Musée de l'Air et de l'Espace in Paris. The linen covering of "Vieux Charles" is very old, which is a large part of the appeal; it was preserved just as Guynemer last saw it. Many other Spads have been painstakingly restored—sometimes several times, resulting in the beautiful examples on display in many of these fine institutions. Some are in near flying condition; the engine of Spad XIII C.1, "Smith IV," housed at the National Air & Space Museum in Washington, DC, could, in theory, be started after minor servicing and being filled with fuel and oil. The Spad XIII at the Owls Head Transportation Museum is on static display in the winter and performs in the museum's flying shows during the summer. The Shannon Air Museum in Fredericksburg, Virginia, is restoring a 1917 Egerton Mann Spad VII to flying condition; it has an original 180 hp Hispano-Suiza engine. If it flies, it will be the only flying original Spad VII with a Hisso in the world. Many of the smaller museums depend on volunteers and donations to keep the doors open, so the next time you visit, please be generous!

The Museum of Flight

The Museum of Flight is located in Seattle, Washington, and museum staff described their institution as follows: "Founded in 1965, the independent, nonprofit Museum of Flight is one of the largest air and space museums in the world, serving 600,000 visitors annually. The museum's collection includes more than 160 historically significant airplanes and spacecraft, from the first fighter plane (1914) to today's 787 Dreamliner. Attractions at the 20-acre, 5-building Seattle campus include the original Boeing Company factory, the NASA Space Shuttle Trainer, and the only exhibit of the rocket engines used to launch Apollo astronauts to the moon. With a foundation of aviation history, the museum is also a hub of news and dialogue with leaders in the emerging field of private spaceflight ventures. The museum's aviation and space library and archives are the largest on the West Coast. More than 150,000 individuals are served annually by the museum's onsite and outreach educational programs. The Museum of Flight is accredited by the American Association of Museums, and is an affiliate of the Smithsonian Institution." *Courtesy of museum website*

The museum's airplane depicts the Blériot-built Spad XIII that was assigned to 1st Lieutenant Norman S. Archibald, United States Air Service, First Pursuit Group, 95th Aero Squadron. A native of Seattle, Archibald flew his first Spad XIII only from June 19, 1918, when it was brand new, until August 10, 1918, when it was destroyed in a takeoff crash at Coulommiers, France. Archibald flew two other Spad XIIIs before being shot down by ground fire and taken prisoner by the Germans on September 8, 1918. In 1935, Archibald recounted his World War I experiences in a bestselling memoir, *Heaven High, Hell Deep. Museum of Flight*

The Museum of Flight's Spad was created by Richard Day of Colonia, New Jersey, and is powered by a Hispano-Suiza, 200-to-235-horsepower, in-line engine and two .303-caliber Vickers machine guns. Because the original Spad drawings were destroyed during World War II, Day had to locate and study existing original examples to build this plane. *Museum of Flight*

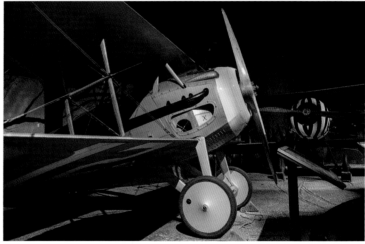

A view of the starboard nose of Archibald's Spad XIII. Archibald returned to military aviation as a captain in the USAF in 1942. *Museum of Flight*

Shannon Air Museum
Fredericksburg, Virginia

Shannon Airport was founded in the 1950s by Sidney Shannon Jr. as part of his love for aviation and to honor his father, Sydney Shannon Sr., who was one of the founders of Eastern Airlines with legendary World War I ace Eddie Rickenbacker. Over the next thirty years the airport became a landmark general-aviation airport in the state of Virginia and beyond. In the mid-1970s, Shannon founded an air museum at his airport that had the largest collection of rare aircraft in the world at the time. The airport had airshows and fly-ins on a regular basis, at which time many of the museum aircraft would be flown. Sidney Shannon Jr. passed away in 1981, and thereafter the aircraft were dispersed and moved to Richmond, Virginia.

During the next thirty years or so, the airport went through many changes. The airport land was owned by developers who had planned to ultimately eliminate the airport and develop the property. In the early 1990s, Billy Toombs, who had worked for Mr. Shannon since the time she was seventeen years old, and Robert Stanley were able to raise money and purchase the airport. The new owners did a great job keeping the airport an airport. However, due to their poor health and the costs associated with running an airport, it became run down and in desperate need of repair.

In 2004, a businessman in Fredericksburg, Virginia, Luke Curtas, started taking flying lessons at Shannon Airport. In April 2006, at the age of forty-four, after going through the flight school at Shannon, he became a private-instrument-rated pilot, who based his aircraft at Shannon.

In 2012, Luke started to talk to Robert and Billy about purchasing the airport. Luke knew about the history of the airport, and he cared for the community in regard to preserving and not losing such a historical part of aviation, and he was also considering the possibility of putting a manufacturing facility on the grass strip located at Shannon. Luke and Kim Curtas purchased Shannon Airport in February 2014.

The old terminal was remodeled and completely restored, as was the ramp for aircraft parking and the parking lot for vehicles. The runway was repaired, and fortunately many of the museum artifacts were never moved to Richmond. With ongoing restoration of the facility, these artifacts were brought out and placed around the terminal. The old hangar, which was attached to the terminal building, was turned into the Robins Nest Café and flight store. Negotiations began with various entities regarding bringing the

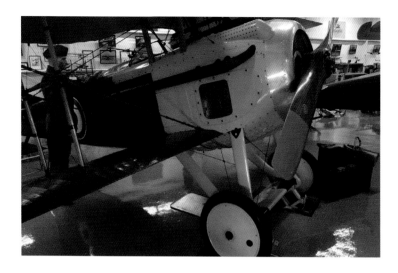

The VAM Spad VII still has its original 180 hp Hispano-Suiza engine. The museum plans to fully restore the aircraft to flying condition and eventually fly it. If they succeed, it will be the only original flying Spad VII in the world. *Shannon Air Museum*

The screened cowling opening characteristic of mid- to late-production Spad VIIs. *Shannon Air Museum*

collection back from Richmond. The big maintenance hangar was completely refurbished and conditioned with humidity control in anticipation of the collection returning home to Shannon. In the early summer of 2016 this dream was realized. *Courtesy of museum website*

The Spad VII (B9913) at the Virginia Air Museum (VAM) was built in 1917 by Mann Egerton & Co. Ltd., in England, as part of nineteen built for the US Army's Rockwell Field Pursuit Gunnery School in San Diego in 1918, to serve as advanced fighter trainers for the US Air Service. In the 1920s, Spads had become obsolete, and as such, B9913 was decommissioned and passed through the hands of several private owners. In 1969, James Ricklef bought the remains of the aircraft and in 1973 completely restored the aircraft to its current iteration. *Shannon Air Museum*

The Wright-Patterson Air Force Museum
Dayton, Ohio

The National Museum of the United States Air Force—the oldest and largest military aviation museum in the world—is located at Wright-Patterson Air Force Base, near Dayton, Ohio. The museum collects, researches, conserves, interprets, and presents the Air Force's history, heritage, and traditions, as well as today's mission to fly, fight, and win . . . in air, space, and cyberspace, to a global audience through engaging exhibits, educational outreach, special programs, and the stewardship of the national historic collection. These statutory duties delegated by the secretary of the Air Force are accomplished on behalf of the American people.

While the majority of the collection is housed at the museum, one-third of the collection is on loan both to civilian and military heritage activities throughout the world. Division personnel work closely with all museum divisions in preserving the historical property collection for research and display. The division manages the Historical Property, Restoration Support, and Unit Memorabilia collections of the United States Air Force. This is in accordance with AFI 84-103 and is achieved through the highest professional standards outlined by the American Alliance of Museums. *Courtesy of museum website*

A Spad VII in colors of the famed *Lafayette Escadrille*—the first Americans to fly and fight for France. This Spad VII was obtained from the Museum of Science and Industry, Chicago, Illinois, and was restored by the 1st Fighter Wing, Selfridge Air Force Base, Michigan, 1962–66.

The Spad XIII of the Museum of the United States Air Force. Built in October 1918 by the Kellner et ses Fils piano works outside Paris, the museum's Spad XIII (serial number 16594) did not see combat. Shipped to the United States with 434 other Spad XIIIs after the Armistice, this aircraft went to San Diego, California, and a smaller, 150 hp Wright-Hispano engine replaced its Hispano-Suiza engine. The museum staff restored this Spad XIII to its original configuration, including a 220 hp Hispano-Suiza engine. It is painted in the markings of America's highest-scoring ace of World War I, with twenty-six victories, Capt. Edward V. Rickenbacker of the 94th Aero Squadron. *USAF*

A close-up of the cowling, showing the twistable fasteners used to secure the cowling and various access panels; by rotating them 90 degrees, the panels can be removed. *USAF*

Technicians working on the rudder framing of the museum's Spad XIII—note that the trailing edge of the rudder is made from linen cord or piano wire. When the fabric covering is shrunk tight, it pulls the wire inward, giving the distinctive scallop contour to the trailing edge. *USAF*

Le Musée de l'Air et de l'Espace

Paris, France

Located within Europe's leading business aviation airport, Paris–Le Bourget, the Museum of Air and Space is one of the world's finest aviation museums, both for the wealth of its collections and long history. It features an incredible collection of more than 400 aircraft, 150 of which are on display: from the very first airplanes to the Breguet 19 "Point d'Interrogation," the Spitfire, and the Concorde. Bridging the past and the future, the prestigious Museum of Air and Space is a lively place, holding events throughout the year, regularly acquiring items for the collection, and hosting activities for all, including Planète Pilote for children and being hired for various events and for filming.

The Museum of Air and Space is also a site museum. In fact, Le Bourget is a place that all aviation heroes have been through, including Charles Lindbergh. It is the birthplace of commercial aviation and includes buildings that are themselves of great cultural interest, such as the terminal building with its art deco architecture.

The museum is open every day except Mondays: between 10:00 am and 6:00 pm from April 1 to September 30, and between 10:00 am and 5:00 pm from October 1 to March 31. *Courtesy of museum website*

Note the rich patina of the spruce interplane struts and their linen cord bindings. Also notice the pushrod that connects the bell crank on the lower wing to the control horn on the aileron. This horn fit into a pocket in the upper wing to allow downward deflection of the control surface. *Roland Turner, Creative Commons Attribution—Share Alike 2.0 Generic license*

The original Spad VII flown by Georges Guynemer—"Vieux Charles"—is one of the feature attractions of this museum. The fabric covering has been preserved in its original condition, which is very evident, although it appears as though the metal work has been restored somewhat. It is fortunate that Guynemer was flying one of his other Spads when he fell, thus allowing his Spad VII to be preserved for posterity. *MarcJP46, Creative Commons Attribution—Share Alike 3.0 Unported license; PpPachy, Creative Commons Attribution—Share Alike 3.0 Unported license*

The time-worn covering of Guynemer's Spad 254 is evident in this image. Note the absence of elevator control wires—the control horn for the elevators was placed near the centerline, which placed it inside the fuselage. This reduced drag and also protected these critical lines from damage. *Roland Turner, Creative Commons Attribution—Share Alike 2.0 Generic license*

The San Diego Air & Space Museum

San Diego, California

Aviation history is truly a remarkable story, and it all unfolds at the San Diego Air & Space Museum. The journey through the history of flight begins as you stand beneath a model of the Montgolfier brothers' hot-air balloon of 1783—the first manned vehicle in recorded history to break the bonds of gravity and lift humans above the Earth. See rare examples of aircraft that suggest the excitement of air combat in the World War I gallery. Marvel at the entertaining and dangerous antics of the barnstormers of the 1920s in the Golden Age of Flight gallery. Mint-condition aircraft in a mint-condition museum—Spitfire Mk. XVI, Navy F6F Hellcat, and A-4 Skyhawk—these beautifully restored airplanes help one appreciate the increasingly complex technology represented in the classic military aircraft of World War II, Korea, and Vietnam. The museum's display of space-age technology, like the desire to journey to the stars, may never be finished; it represents an adventure that the human race has truly just begun.

From a small one-hangar beginning, the San Diego Air & Space Museum's annex at Gillespie Field has grown to become an integral part of the museum's aircraft restoration and replica reproduction program. Staffed mainly by volunteers, the facility has produced some of SDASM's finest work.

Of local significance, restoration of a Convair F-102A Delta Dagger was recently completed at the annex. This aircraft was built in San Diego at Convair's Lindbergh Field plant in the mid-1950s. *Courtesy of museum website*

The museum's Spad VII was manufactured in Norwich, England, in 1917. Later that year, it was sold to the United States and was one of many sent to Rockwell Field on North Island in San Diego. While there, the Spad VIIs, retaining their British markings, were used for advanced fighter training and took part in the huge Armistice celebration flyover of downtown San Diego in 1919. The Spad went through several subsequent owners.

In 1981, this aircraft was purchased by the San Diego Air & Space Museum at auction from the Wings and Wheels Museum in Orlando, Florida. The museum began restoration of the Spad in 1990 with a team of volunteer craftsmen and expert consultants, including noted antique aircraft authorities Jim and Zona Appleby, who were enlisted to restore the fuselage, empennage, instruments, and engine at their home in Yucca Valley, California. Restoration of the wings and painting and assembly were done by volunteers working at the museum's Gillespie Field facility in El Cajon, California. The aircraft is 95 percent original, making it one of the most authentic World War I aircraft in existence. *SDASM*

The National Air & Space Museum
Washington, DC

The Smithsonian's National Air & Space Museum (NASM) maintains the world's largest and most significant collection of aviation and space artifacts, encompassing all aspects of human flight, as well as related works of art and archival materials. It operates two landmark facilities that, together, welcome more than eight million visitors a year, making it the most visited museum in the country. It also is home to the Center for Earth and Planetary Studies.

The Smithsonian's National Air & Space Museum collects, preserves, studies, and exhibits artifacts, archival materials, and works of art related to the history, culture, and science of aviation and spaceflight and the study of the universe. Its research and outreach activities serve all audiences, within and beyond its walls. The museum commemorates the past and is committed to educating and inspiring people to foster appreciation for the importance of flight to humanity. *Courtesy of museum website*

The NASM Spad flown by A. R. Brooks-Smith IV, outside the Garber facility shortly after restoration in the 1970s. This is one of my favorite photos due to its unpretentiousness; you can almost smell the dope drying in the late fall afternoon! *NASM*

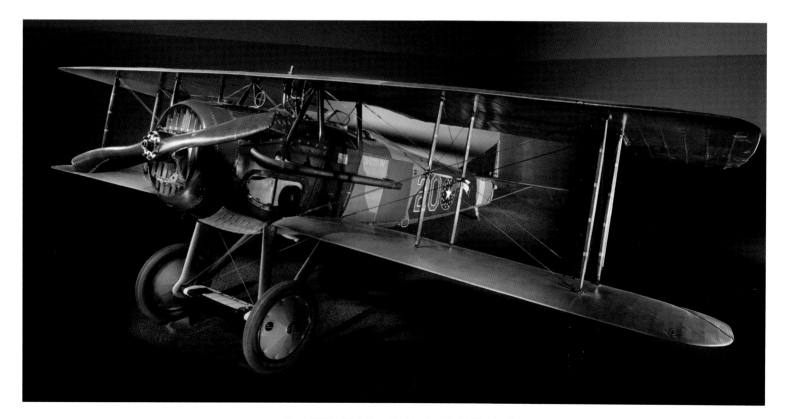

Spad XIII Smith IV installed in the World War I gallery at the NASM in Washington, DC. *NASM2016-01774*

The Udvar-Hazy Center
Chantilly, Virginia

The Udvar-Hazy Center in Chantilly, Virginia, is the companion facility to the NASM, on the National Mall in Washington, DC. Opened in 2003, its two huge hangars—the Boeing Aviation Hangar and the James S. McDonnell Space Hangar—display thousands of aviation and space artifacts, including a Lockheed SR-71 Blackbird, a Concorde, and the space shuttle *Discovery*. The Udvar-Hazy Center is also home to the Mary Baker Engen Restoration Hangar, where preservation of the NASM's collections takes place. A glassed-in mezzanine provides a view of restoration projects in progress. Researchers will also find the majority of the archives' collections at the Udvar-Hazy Center reading room. The Hazy center is home to the Spad XVI described in chapter 5.

The Brussels Air Museum
Brussels, Belgium

The wealth and diversity of the collections presented in the Royal Museum of the Armed Forces and Military History attract surprise and admiration from Belgium's compatriots as well as from the many foreign visitors. Moreover, the Air and Space Section has had a fast and very successful development, thanks to the long-term vision of a few military and civilian airman and ground crew who created, roughly forty years ago, the Association AELR. These volunteers, former members of the Belgian air force and Sabena, or simply aviation fanatics, devoted their time and energy to gather and refurbish the displayed aircraft and the many other air-related items. Thanks to the enthusiasm and the dynamism of these volunteers, among whom are retired senior pilot-officers Mike Terlinden and Hervé Donnet and warrant-officer Jean Booten of the Belgian air force, an air museum that is proud of its name is presented to the public. Today the restoration activities are assumed by crews of volunteers and members of the AELR and are regrouped in a restoration entity. Each crew is in charge of a specific airplane. To deal with more-complex technical problems and for infrastructure works, the museum fortunately benefits from the support of the Belgian air force and the community services. *Courtesy of museum website*

This Spad XIII of the Brussels Air Museum (SP49) never saw combat, but perhaps for this reason it has survived. The identification number was painted inside the cockpit on one of the aluminum panels. However, the airplane is assembled from parts of other airplanes, all constructed by Adolphe Bernard: fin, from 8949; tailplane and elevators, 7971; lower wings, 8919; and upper wing, 8865. BAM staff note that during World War I and just after, many aircraft were assembled from parts of many different aircraft. *Ad Meskens / wikimedia commons*

Pictured is SP8949 in 1918 at Evere, Belgium. In the background is a Nieuport 10; one can only wonder at what other treasures lurk in the hangar, and how many of them are still around today. *BAM*

The Italian Air Force Museum
Museo Storico Aeronautica Militare
Vigna di Valle, Italy

Translated and paraphrased from the museum website: "The collection of Italian pieces is displayed inside four large hangars built on the western side of Bracciano Lake, next to the sports complex of the Italian air force, in the old seaplane station of Vigna di Valle, the oldest Italian aviation site, a location that became the first experimental aviation shipyard. It was here that the first Italian military airship, the N.1, was built in 1908 by Crocco and Ricaldoni. Later, the airport served as the Experimental Seaplane and Naval Armament Centre up until 1945. It was the headquarters of the 88th Maritime Fighter Group, and after the war it became the Search and Rescue Command, home for the 84th Seaplane Group. The exhibition halls depict the history of Italian aviation, from the origins of flight (with the sketches of Leonardo da Vinci), to the monoplanes used in World Wars I and II, to the present."

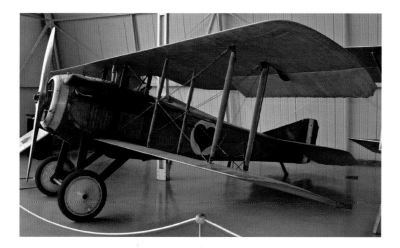

Ernesto Cabruna flew this Spad VII. Cabruna was credited with eight victories and was awarded the Silver Medal for Military Valor at the end of 1917 and the Gold Medal for Military Valor in 1918 . His Spad VII bears *77a Squadriglia* insignia (the red heart on a white spot), as well as Cabruna's personal markings—the coat of arms of his native city, Tortona. His aircraft appears to be preserved in near-original condition. Note the louvered cowl opening, indicating a late-production Spad VII.
Alan Wilson, Creative Commons Attribution—Share Alike 2.0 Generic license

CHAPTER 9

Replica Flying Spads

There is only one original Spad currently flying, and it is in the collection of Memorial Flight in France. It is a Spad XIII C.1 and is part of their regular flying show. The few other Spads scattered across the globe are replicas. Replicas have a big advantage over originals, since they can take advantage of newer materials and engines, and, most importantly, if the aircraft is damaged, it can easily be repaired, and it is not like losing a piece of history as with an original 1916–18 artifact. Interestingly, I know of two replicas that have been built in the last five years—a Spad XIII in the colors of James Norman Hall of the famed *Lafayette Escadrille* at the Vintage Aero Museum in Colorado, and a Spad XIII that is being built currently at the Golden Age Air Museum in Bethel, Pennsylvania; this Spad XIII will be finished in the markings of

Charles J. Biddle, commanding officer of the 13th Aero Squadron. Replicas are also immensely appealing in that someone who has never seen a Spad fly can go to an airshow at Old Rhinebeck Aerodrome in New York, the Golden Age Aerodrome in Pennsylvania, or Vintage Aero in Colorado and see a Spad in its natural element—the sky. There is nothing more exhilarating than seeing one of these canvas-and-spruce raptors of the Great War power up and gently break ground—ascending into great fleecy clouds on a warm summer's afternoon—the smell of cut grass and castor oil perfuming the air. The following pages depict the aerodromes across the world, where visitors can see Spads fly as part of airshows. Do yourself and your family a favor: make the trek to one of these enclaves; you won't regret it.

Old Rhinebeck Aerodrome

Red Hook, New York

Cole Palen founded the Old Rhinebeck Aerodrome (ORA) in 1958 with a handful of airplanes and a dream. He built it into a world-renowned destination as America's first flying museum of antique aircraft. The Rhinebeck Aerodrome Museum was established in 1993 as a 501(c)(3) nonprofit organization to continue Cole's legacy. Their mission is preserving, restoring, and flying the aircraft of the pioneer, World War I, and golden ages of aviation.

Over sixty vintage aircraft, many antique automobiles and motorcycles, and related memorabilia are located in a classic small-town-airport setting. The static display museum is open from May through October, and two different airshows are flown each Saturday and Sunday, mid-June through mid-October.

ORA consists of a volunteer board of trustees, professional staff, and many volunteers who do everything from restorations to mowing the runway. *Courtesy of ORA website*

Old Rhinebeck Aerodrome has the only flying Spad VII replica in the United States. Originally, it was finished as Georges Guynemer's "Vieux Charles" of *Escadrille 3*, or the "Storks," and it is a favorite sight at their airshows, which run from May through October. It does not have a Hisso engine, however, but a Continental, and an appropriately smaller prop. *ORA*

This season, ORA decided to overhaul the Spad VII with a refurbished engine, new prop, and new paint scheme. The aircraft now depicts George Turnure's Spad VII from the *Lafayette Escadrille*. Turnure was officially credited with 1.5 victories—both balloons and both in 1918.

Golden Age Air Museum
Bethel, Pennsylvania

The Golden Age Air Museum was established in 1997, and its mission is to entertain visitors and educate them about the early days of aviation through its special events and daily operations. The museum offers the chance to explore the past, learn how and what the early aviators flew, and discover the lost art of early aircraft construction. Museum displays include full-size operational aircraft and automobiles, as well as displays of artifacts from aviation's golden age. Craftsmen are continually working on restoring new additions for the collection, and this work is done in view of visitors. Talk with the restoration volunteers and learn techniques and practices of early aircraft builders. The museum is a nonprofit 501(c)(3) organization and receives its financial support through donations, admission fees, and membership donations. GAAM is officially open May 1 through the end of October. Please visit their website for more information about flying shows and events: www.goldenageair.org

Six to eight dedicated volunteers are building a replica Spad XIII at the Golden Age Air Museum in Bethel, Pennsylvania. Pictured at right, volunteers Gerry Wild and Rob Waring are seen working on the horizontal stabilizer. Museum director Paul Dougherty is in the background.. It will depict Charles Biddle's Spad of the 13th Aero Squadron. Biddle was a Pennsylvania native and was one of the few pilots in the US Army Air Service to fly a Spad XII. Work on the Spad continues, and the hope is that it'll be flying sometime during 2019. Mike O'Neill described the Spad as a difficult airplane to build—one that requires exacting craftsmanship, patience, and dedication. Many donations have helped make this project a reality, including sponsors for wing ribs.

This image depicts the lower port wing panel and fuselage with a color overlay of what the finished aircraft will resemble when eventually covered and painted. *GAAM*

The sheet-metal work for the Spad cowling was done completely by hand by museum director Paul Dougherty. He used various metalworking mallets and shot-filled sandbags to achieve the proper compound curves. Moreover, the cowling required artful "stretching" of its length by about 4 inches (when compared to original Spads) to accommodate the modern Continental 0-470 engine. Since the Continental is a six-cylinder engine and the original Hisso had eight, the exhaust stack had to be carefully crafted to include the four exhaust points to look right; however, only one of them is serving as an actual exhaust from the Continental. In the image of the Spad's tail, Mike O'Neal is seen carefully applying varnish to the delicate framing of the Spad's rudder. *GAAM*

Two views of the cockpit nearing completion—the Spad XIII had a variety of instruments, and the replica loosely follows the instrumentation seen on Smith IV at NASM. The GAAM replica features an original Jaeger tachometer, clock (*center*), and altimeter (*seen to right in the leather casing*). Since the replica has a modern engine and an electrical system, these instruments are hidden to the casual observer but are still accessible to the pilot. Another nod to modern times is the fuel tank; the original Spads had a belly tank that required a fuel pump; since this was a bit convoluted, the GAAM replica will have its fuel tank where the ammunition magazines would have been. One method GAAM helped to fund this project was by allowing the public to "buy a rib," seen pictured here. For a price, a person could sign his/her name to a rib used in the actual airplane. They received a picture of the rib, as well as a diagram of where exactly their rib is placed in the overall airframe—a very good idea! *GAAM*

Owls Head Transportation Museum
Owls Head, Maine

Founded in 1974, the Owls Head Transportation Museum (OHTM) is an operating, nonprofit museum with a strong focus on educational initiatives. Located on the Maine coast near the Knox County Regional Airport, the museum is a place where machines of a bygone era are celebrated through conservation, preservation, and demonstration.

Unlike many transportation museums, the OHTM operates their collection of aircraft, ground vehicles, and engines at a number of special events conducted throughout the year. Care and maintenance of these historic vehicles require the attention of a large volunteer workforce that, under the supervision of a professional staff, ensures that the collection is in operating condition. While the museum is open all year, the summer event season offers an unparalleled opportunity to see the collection in action during scheduled airshows and ground vehicle demonstrations. *Courtesy of museum website*

OHTM has a Spad XIII replica that flies in the summer months and is displayed during the winter. It is finished in the striking checkerboard pattern of the 94th Aero Squadron (nicknamed "Hat in Ring") made famous by Eddie Rickenbacker—America's Ace of Aces. It is powered by a 180 hp Lycoming "flat four" engine, instead of the 220 hp Hisso that was standard in the Spad XIII. The reduction in power makes the aircraft "tricky at slow speeds." The original livery for the aircraft was a more traditional camouflage paint scheme, with the markings of Rickenbacker's plane. *All images courtesy of OHTM*

The Vintage Aero Flying Museum

Ft. Lupton, Colorado

The Lafayette Foundation is named in honor of the men who served in the *Lafayette Escadrille* and the Lafayette Flying Corps (LFC) during World War I. At the final reunion of the LFC, organized by Dr. James J. Parks in 1983, its surviving members, headed by Reginald Sinclair, asked Jim Parks and his son, Andy, to "carry on the Corps" after they were gone, passing the charter onto the Parks family. In their honor, the name of the museum was changed to the Lafayette Foundation.

Today, Andy Parks, as the president and executive director of the Vintage Aero Flying Museum, home of the Lafayette Foundation, continues the work of his father, and grandfather, to preserve the history and memory of the men and women who have served their countries via aviation both in peacetime and wartime, for the benefit of future generations to come. *Courtesy of museum website*

Andy Parks, of Vintage Aero Flying Museum in Ft. Lupton, Colorado, has built and recently flown a replica Spad XIII finished in James Norman Hall's colors. This is an interesting airplane in that it features the original rounded wingtips on early-production Spad XIIIs. It was built by Andy and his dedicated team of friends and volunteers. Among this talented group are Mark Holliday, Mike Gulerer, Kenny Rice, and Robert Simpson; behind him is Jerry Roy—who did all metal fabrication on the cowl. Mark Holliday test-flew the Spad and reported that it flew very well indeed! *Images courtesy of author and VAFM*

The Vintage Aero Museum's beautiful replica of Jimmy Hall's Spad XIII pictured at right. James Norman Hall was a writer and fighter pilot who served in the *Lafayette Escadrille* during World War I. After the Armistice, he made a solo flight along the entire length of the Western Front to see it from the air one last time. On this flight he decided to abandon Western "civilization" in favor of moving to Tahiti—a place where war was a foreign concept. Here he and his writing partner Charles Nordhoff wrote the classic *Mutiny on the Bounty*—the story of Fletcher Christian, who also turned his back on civilization to live in peace on a remote Pacific Island. *VAM*

Bibliography

Bruce, J. M. *Spad 7.C1*. Berkhamsted, UK: Albatros Productions, 1988.

Connors, John F. *Spad Fighters in Action*. Carrollton, TX: Squadron/Signal, 1989.

Guttman, Jon. *Spad XIII vs. Fokker D VII: Western Front 1918*. Oxford: Osprey, 2009.

Hall, James Norman. *My Island Home*. Boston: Little, Brown, 1952.

Hare, Robert C. "Bechereau and His Spads." *Popular Aviation* 21, no. 5 (November 1937): 34–36.

Kowalski, Tomasz J. *Spad S.A.1–VII.C1*. Lublin, Poland: Kagero, 2007.

"The Spad Scout." *Flight*, August 16, 1917.

Tallman, Frank. *Flying the Old Planes*. New York: Doubleday, 1973.

Velek, Martin. *Spad S. VII C1*. Prague: Mark I, 2004.